EVOLUTION
THE WHOLE LIFE-ON-EARTH STORY

Glenn Murphy wrote his first book, *Why Is Snot Green?*, while working at the Science Museum, London. Since then he has written around twenty popular-science titles aimed at kids and teens, including the bestselling *How Loud Can You Burp?* and *Space: The Whole Whizz-Bang Story*.

These days he lives in sunny, leafy North Carolina — with his wife Heather, his son Sean, and two *unfeasibly* large felines.

Also by Glenn Murphy

BODIES: THE WHOLE BLOOD-PUMPING STORY

SPACE: THE WHOLE WHIZZ-BANG STORY

SUPERGEEK! DINOSAURS, BRAINS AND SUPERTRAINS

SUPERGEEK! ROBOTS, SPACE AND FURRY ANIMALS

WHY IS SNOT GREEN?
And other extremely important questions
(and answers) from the Science Museum

HOW LOUD CAN YOU BURP?
And other extremely important questions
(and answers) from the Science Museum

STUFF THAT SCARES YOUR PANTS OFF!
The Science Museum Book of Scary Things
(and ways to avoid them)

DOES FARTING MAKE YOU FASTER?
And other extremely important questions (and answers)
about sport from the Science Museum

WILL FARTS DESTROY THE PLANET?
And other extremely important questions (and answers)
about climate change from the Science Museum

POO! WHAT *IS* THAT SMELL?
Everything you ever needed to know about the five senses

SCIENCE
SORTED

WHOA!

C. DARWIN ESQ.

YOUR GREAT-
GREAT-GREAT-
GREAT-GREAT-
UNCLE GEOFF

EVOLUTION
THE WHOLE LIFE-ON-EARTH STORY

UGG

UGGG

How
VULGAR

GLENN MURPHY

Illustrated by Mike Phillips

MACMILLAN CHILDREN'S BOOKS

To Sean Joseph Murphy — evolving rapidly since 2012

Some material in this book has previously been published in 2010
by Macmillan Children's Books in *Evolution, Nature and Stuff*

This edition published 2014 by Macmillan Children's Books
a division of Macmillan Publishers Limited
20 New Wharf Road, London N1 9RR
Basingstoke and Oxford
Associated companies throughout the world
www.panmacmillan.com

ISBN 978-1-4472-5460-7

1 3 5 7 9 8 6 4 2

A CIP catalogue record for this book is available from the British Library.

Printed and bound by CPI Group (UK) Ltd, Croydon CRO 4YY

CONTENTS

WHAT'S LIFE ALL ABOUT?

Oooh. That's a biggie! Not sure I can answer that. Come to think of it, I'm not sure I even have that one figured out myself yet . . .

Hold on – I didn't mean that. I mean, you know, life and living things. Life's supposed to be about evolution, and living things evolve, right? But what makes something alive in the first place? What actually is life?

Ahh – now that's a good question. Life, in some ways, is still a mystery. We know that life on Earth began over 3.6 billion years ago, a little more than a billion years after the planet itself was formed.

It took a wee while to get started, then?

Right. But once it did it was off like the clappers.

What do you mean?

Well, we know that life began with simple, microscopic creatures no more complex than a few chemicals in a fatty ball. And we know that from there life developed into everything from seaweed and sharks to trees, toadstools and tyrannosaurs. A few million years later, we had large mammals, monkeys and apes. And it wasn't too long after that the first humans hit the scene.

So life on Earth has developed from little fatty balls floating in a murky sea to farmers, artists, engineers, scientists, philosophers, presidents, pop stars and reality TV contestants. Not bad.

Some scientists question whether this last group represents a real step forward from bacteria. I think perhaps not.

3

Wow — that is quite a jump.

In a way, yes. But you also have to remember that the whole path from bacteria to Britney Spears took billions of years to trudge. With a couple of hundred years of biology — the study of life — under our belts, we're now fairly sure of how most of this came about, and how long it all took to happen. Living things evolved from simple to complex in a series of tiny steps taking millions of years each, steered by natural processes of life, death and change.

LESSON 1: WHAT'S FOR BREAKFAST?

Get It Sorted – What is Biology?

Biology is, literally, 'the study (or science) of life'. Humans have been watching and studying wildlife for as long as they've been around to do it, but the modern science of biology didn't begin until the seventeenth or eighteenth century.

Our early human ancestors observed the natural world around them learning what plants they could and couldn't eat, and how to hunt large animals for food.

Over time they experimented with keeping animals for food and growing plants near their permanent homes (this was the beginning of a new age of farming).

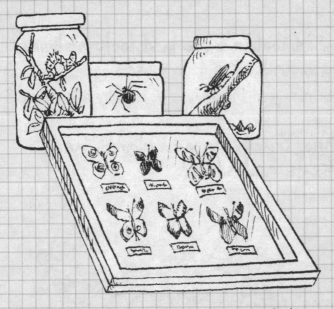

The things-in-jars stuff only started a couple of hundred years ago with amateur collectors and observers of the living world who called themselves naturalists or natural philosophers. They collected living things in jars, sketched them artfully in journals, and started to sort them and name them. They also cut dead things up to find out how their bodies were put together and occasionally came up with a theory for why something looked or behaved the way it did.

Then, at some time in the nineteenth century, the study of the natural world went from being a pastime or hobby to being an official science. Real biology (and real science in general) is not just about looking and collecting. It's also about thinking, testing and figuring things out.

There's one thing we need to decide before we set off on our global safari: which things should we look at, and which should we skip?

Er . . . shouldn't we just look at living things, and skip the rest?

Okay. Sounds good. But what do we mean by 'living things'?

I dunno. Bacteria and plants and monkeys and stuff.

Okay . . . and 'the rest'?

Well . . . all the other stuff. You know, rocks . . . soil . . . islands . . . underpants. Stuff like that.

Sounds reasonable enough. But while these things are not alive in themselves, many rocks and soils are positively teeming with life, and some islands are built entirely from living organisms. (And believe me, you don't want to know how many things are living in your underpants right now.)

Really?

Yep. Just because you can't see or recognize them right away, that doesn't mean they're not alive. Living things come in an enormously wide variety of shapes, sizes and forms, many of which were — until fairly recently — not really thought of as alive at all. So we can hardly set about defining life before we can all agree on *what's alive* and *what isn't*.

Alive - or Not?

Look at the list of things below, and sort them into two groups – alive **(A)** and not alive **(B)**. I've done the first two for you.

Toothbrush

Mountain

Mud

Mould

Jellyfish

Mushrooms

Tree

River

Bacteria

Sponge

Coral reef

A	B
Monkey	Rock

Only **five** things on the list were **not** actually living things. See the bottom of the page for the correct answers.

While the sponge in your bathroom may not be alive, there are entire families of living sponges in the ocean. Many of these sit on coral reefs — which may look like big, undersea rock piles, but are, in fact, animals too!

And the mould on your bathroom tiles (or furring up that half-eaten tub of baked beans in the fridge), well that's a type of fungus, and it's alive too.

No way! I thought living things had to ... you know ... move and do stuff.

Well, they all **do stuff**, but not all of them **move** that much. Think about it — most trees and plants remain stationary for life, save for a bit of upward growth. And, on the flipside, icebergs and rivers move, and no one would say that they're alive, right?

These things are not alive: **rock, toothbrush, mountain, river** and **mud**. All the rest are alive.

Err . . . right. I s'pose so. So, if living things can look like lifeless ones, how do we decide which is which?

Gooooood question. To help us out with that, biologists have come up with a list of features that all living things must have. A kind of 'life list'. Basically, if they have all these features, they're alive; if not, they're not. Simple. So here they are:

Life List

1 **Living things self-organize.** They arrange themselves into bodies and structures. This can be as simple as the fatty bubble surrounding the watery chemical core of a bacterium. Or as complex as the bones, guts and muscles of a racehorse. What's important is that **living things sort themselves out.**

2 **Living things reproduce**. They make copies of themselves, which in turn make copies of themselves, and gradually grow in number to create an entire *colony* or *species*.

3 **Living things eat stuff.** Or, rather, they absorb chemicals and minerals from their environment and turn them into either **a)** bits of their bodies or **b)** energy to power all that eating, organizing and reproducing.

4 **Living things change things.** You know when living organisms have been around, because they alter their surroundings. Largely as a result of all that organizing, reproducing and eating . . .

5 **Living things have life-cycles.** They show predictable, programmed patterns that take them from the beginning to the end of their lives – through birth, growth, reproduction and death.

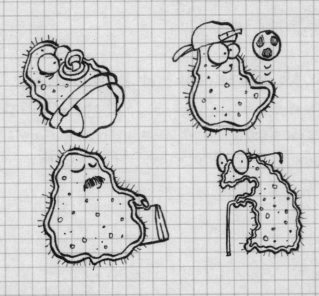

Now if you go back and look at the As and Bs in *your* list on page 8 once more, you'll see how much easier it is to recognize the living and the non-living. Mountains may seem to grow (over time), and rivers can alter their environments by carving out canyons. But neither one of these actually eats things* or reproduces.

*Except, perhaps, the occasional mountain climber or canoeing enthusiast.

Corals, mushrooms and moulds may all just sit there *looking* lifeless. But in fact they all self-organize, eat, reproduce, alter their surroundings and follow repeating lifecycles.

Wow. Never thought of it like that.

So, now we know what to look for, it's time to set off and explore the planet. Hmmmm . . . but where should we start? With so many living things in the world, it's hard to know where to begin . . .

Couldn't we just start with antelopes and finish up with zebras?

Ahh, but then we'll only cover the animals. Plus you've already skipped aardvarks, aardwolves and anteaters.

Oh.

On the other hand, you're right — we can't just wade in there without a plan. If we're going to tackle a whole world full of living things, we need some way of sorting them all out first. Thankfully, there's a science that lets us do just that. Zoology.

So we're starting at the zoo, then?

In a way, yes. So grab your sunblock and a pair of good walking shoes. We're off to explore every nook and cranny of the living world...

Back-garden Biology

You can start your global life-safari in your neighbourhood. Have a go at being a biologist with these activities:

Pond sampling – clean out an empty jam jar and use it to scoop a water sample from your local pond. Then look at drops of it under a magnifying glass (or, better still, microscope) and count how many water fleas and other bugs you can see.

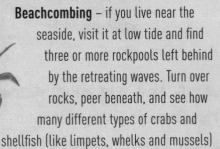

Beachcombing – if you live near the seaside, visit it at low tide and find three or more rockpools left behind by the retreating waves. Turn over rocks, peer beneath, and see how many different types of crabs and shellfish (like limpets, whelks and mussels) you can find. Also, comb the beach for shells, crab skeletons, seaweed and shark-egg cases ('mermaid's purses').

See how many different plant and animal species you can identify from the evidence.

Birdwatching - grab a friend or family member, a pair of binoculars and a guidebook detailing the birds in your area (preferably one with lots of pictures). Then head into a local wood, forest or meadow. See how many bird species you can spot during a one-hour walk.

What's the big deal about evolution?

Charles Darwin's theory of evolution was the first scientific theory to explain the appearance and behaviour of not just some, but all living species. It told us *how all living things were related*. As if that wasn't enough, it also explained the origin of new species, why some species become *extinct*, and the reason for the great variety of living species on the planet.

The 'environment' can change in many different ways, and animal groups don't necessarily have to be physically separated (say, by mountains or rivers) in order to form new species. Sometimes a change in depth, diet, weather or the habits of choosy female animals can be enough to do it.

Darwin's Theory of Evolution

1 Living things, even within a species, vary in appearance and behaviour. Individual animals may be bigger or smaller, faster or slower, more or less attractive, more or less intelligent. This is called natural variation.

2 Depending on the time and place (climate, amount of food available, number of nasty predators around, etc.), some members of this species will be better able to survive (or have more babies) than others.

3 Therefore, the animals best suited to their surroundings will have more babies, while those less well suited will either die or fail to reproduce. This is called natural selection.

4 Over time, this means all surviving members of a species will end up looking like those 'best suited' winners, as they will be the only ones left around. (At least until the environment changes.) This effect has been nicknamed 'survival of the fittest'.

5 If two groups of animals from a single species are separated, and find themselves in different environments, then each group will evolve to fit its own environment – just as described above. Eventually, the two groups will become so different that they form two separate species. This is how new species are created.

So how did Darwin come up with the idea in the first place? Did he just dream it up one day?

Actually, the idea of evolution had been around for quite a few years beforehand. And, as some of the history books say, he didn't come up with the whole idea during his famous round-the-world voyage on board the *Beagle* (if you haven't heard about that, don't worry — there's more on that in a minute).

Instead, he figured it out gradually, over many years, and kept his ideas to himself. Only when someone else threatened to beat him to the finish-line did he write his famous book . . . which changed the face of science forever.

Darwin's Voyage Around the World

From December 1831 to October 1836, Darwin sailed right around the world on board a ship called the *Beagle* — invited as a 'gentleman companion' for the ship's map-making captain, Robert FitzRoy. But he later appointed himself **ship's naturalist** and began sending samples of the plants, animals and fossils he found back to London for later study.

In **Argentina**, Darwin found some mysterious fossils. These turned out to be **giant ground sloths** and **American camels** that had long since become extinct.

Later, he discovered a tiny, endangered species of South American ostrich called a **rhea**. Actually, he and the captain unknowingly ate one, after locals captured and cooked it.

WHY WOULD GOD CREATE A SPECIES JUST TO LET IT BE DESTROYED?

That particular species is now extinct, partly thanks to the crew of the Beagle. Thankfully, two other rhea species managed to avoid being eaten to extinction, and still survive today.

And that wasn't the only endangered species Darwin and the captain ate on that trip. Still, being a good scientist (if not a great conservationist), Darwin kept the bones and sent them to London anyway.

While Darwin trekked through the rainforests of **Peru** he was dumbstruck by the huge variety of plants, trees, birds, insects, monkeys and other animals on display.

IF ALL SPECIES WERE CREATED FOR MAN'S BENEFIT, WHY WOULD GOD CREATE SO MANY WONDERFUL PLANTS AND ANIMALS AND HIDE THEM SO FAR OUT OF SIGHT?

On its way west across the Pacific Ocean, the *Beagle* landed briefly on an isolated set of islands 600 miles (1,000 km) west of Ecuador, known as the **Galapagos Islands.**

Here, too, Darwin discovered an incredible variety of animal life, including giant, lumbering tortoises and scary-looking marine iguanas – perched like dragons or dinosaurs on rocks near the shore.

Among these many species, Darwin also sketched, collected and labelled dozens of bird species previously unknown to naturalists. He sent them back to a friend in London to identify them – labelling them, as best he knew, as finches, wrens, thrushes and woodpeckers.

Years later, once he was back in England with his family, Darwin's bird-expert friend told him that they were all, in fact, types of finch – now known as **Galapagos finches**. They just looked like other bird families because of their different body sizes and beak shapes.

EACH SPECIES OF FINCH HAS ADAPTED IN ORDER TO EAT DIFFERENT THINGS...

Finches with parrot-like beaks cracked nuts, while those with thin, woodpecker-like beaks probed trees for insects, and so on. The birds with beaks best suited to the local food sources had survived and reproduced, while those with less ideal beak shapes had died off – leaving a range of different finch species that had evolved from a single 'ancestor'.

So after all that he told everyone all about it, right?

Nope. Back at home he studied other living things – like barnacles, orchids and domestic dog breeds – that made him think again and again about his theory. And he continued to compile notes and write essays for himself. But he never spoke openly about his ideas, much less published them. Not for over two decades.

Arrghhhh!

What? Why not?

Partly because he knew that the idea of evolution would be thought of as ridiculous, or even dangerous, and he feared for his reputation. At that time most people thought that God had created all living things at once, and placed them perfectly throughout the world. Darwin knew that some people would think it was blasphemy (or insulting to God and the Church) to say otherwise. So he waited and waited – collecting facts and making notes to himself.

Sigh.
So when did he finally come out with it?

In 1858, when a younger man named Alfred Russel Wallace wrote to him, telling him of his own theories of evolution. Inspired by the travel tales of Darwin and other naturalists, Wallace had embarked on his own round-the-world journey. In Malaysia he noticed the similarities between two classes

In particular, between the mammals found from Borneo northwards, and the marsupials found further south.

of mammals separated by the geography of the islands. From this, he deduced – much as Darwin did with his finches – that even quite different mammal species would develop to look like each other if their environments and needs were very similar.

Darwin panicked, thinking Wallace would beat him to the punch, got his many decades' worth of notes together and published as soon as he could. The book —

SCRITCH! SCRATCH!

On the Origin of Species

— became one of the most famous, influential and controversial books of all time.

Whoa.

I knew evolution was supposed to be important and stuff. But I didn't realize it was that big a deal.

It really was. And it still is.

Of course there's still a great deal that we don't understand. But thanks to Darwin we know a lot more than we did. And as for the rest, we can now make more educated (and hopefully more accurate) guesses.

That's pretty good going, I s'pose.

Yep — not bad at all. Nice one, Charlie!

A Chimp by Any Other Name

How do animals get their names?

Every animal has at least two names. Their common name —
like 'gorilla', 'emu' and 'tiger' — is often given by local people in
the areas where the animals live. But they also have an official
scientific name, given to them by biologists or zoologists.
And it's not just animal species that get their own posh
technical title. Plants, fungi, bacteria and all other living
things get them too.

But how did people decide what to call them in the first place?

Did some African guy just point at a gorilla once and say 'gorilla' ... and everyone agreed?

Possibly, yes. In some cases the animal's common name is very ancient, and may have been around since human tribes first began speaking and naming them. The word 'gorilla' comes

from the ancient African word *gorillai*, which the people of West Africa were using as early as 480 BC, and had probably been using for thousands of years before that. Other common names describe the animal in some

Orang-utan

way in the native language. *Orang-utan*, for example, means 'old man of the forest' in Malay. And *koala*, interestingly, means 'no drink' in some Australian aboriginal tongues.

Koala

Koalas get all the water they need from raindrops and dewdrops on the moist leaves they eat. The clever aborigines noticed this, and named it accordingly.

So do all animal names mean something like that?

Not all of them. Some locals probably chose names for the animals at random, while their languages were still fairly new. But in fact many (or most) animals were named by explorers and scholars from distant countries.

The English name 'sloth', for example, means 'laziness', but the native tribes of South America know the animal as a *rit* or *ritto* (meaning 'sleeper'). Similarly, *aardvark* means 'earth pig' in Afrikaans,

hippopotamus means 'river horse' in Greek,

and 'giraffe' comes from the Arabic word *zirafah*, meaning 'the tallest of them all'.

Many animal names, in fact, owe more to the books and travels of English, Dutch, Greek and Arab scholars and sailors than they do to local tribes.

What about the posh science-y name? How does an animal get one of those?

The scientific name for a species is usually given in Latin or Greek — the old-school languages of science (and learning in general). In the old days, this allowed scholars from all over the world to understand each other without learning loads of new languages. And while scientists now tend to use English or other languages instead, the habit for naming animals in Greek or Latin has stuck around. Partly because it also simplifies things when a single species has more than one common name.

Get It Sorted – How to Name a Species

The official name normally has two parts. These could describe the physical features of the species, and/or where you can find it.

polar bear — *Ursus maritimus*
('sea bear' — since it swims so well between ice floes of the Arctic)
American black bear — *Ursus americanus*
('American bear')

Sometimes an animal may be named after the person who discovered it, or even after famous scientists and celebrities.

It's not just animals who get a double-barrelled scientific name: plants, fungi, bacteria and protists (single-celled organisms) do too.

Berberis darwinii — Darwin's barberry
Rhinoderma darwinii — Darwin's frog
Calponia harrisonfordi — a type of spider
Agra schwarzeneggeri — a type of beetle

Animal Anagrams

Unravel the anagrams, and translate these scientific animal names into common ones.

Scientific name	Meaning
Spilogale poturius	'stinking spotty weasel'
Orcinus orca	'killer-from-hell whale'
Ursus arctos horribilis	'horrible-bear bear'
Macropus rufus	'red big-foot'
Ornithorhynchus anatinus	'duck-like, bird-snout'
Ailuropoda melanoleuci	'black-and-white cat-foot'

So scientists just call the animals whatever they want, then? As long as it's in Greek or Latin?

Not quite. There's a bit more to it than that. While the two-part names of a new genus or species can be chosen fairly freely the full name of a species can contain twenty or more

Common name	Common name (anagram)
....	desk stunk top
....	leek war hill
....	barry leg ziz
....	radar ken goo
....	tacky billed sud pulp
....	aid gnat nap

(answers on page 162)

parts, and describes which higher group, class and family the animal belongs to. In fact, the full name describes a species all the way down to the kingdom (animal, plant, fungal, protist or bacterial) that it belongs to.

A very clever Swedish naturalist called **Carl** (or **Carolus**) **Linnaeus** first came up with this system back in 1735. He wrote a book called *Systema Naturae* ('natural systems'), in which he began to classify all living things into higher

groupings and families, and spent most of his life rewriting and building upon this work. The groupings he used have changed a bit since then (some new ones have been added, while others have been dropped). But biologists still use pretty much the same system of classifying and naming living things today — almost 300 years later.

Here's how it works:
Each **species** is part of a larger **genus**, and each **genus** is part of an even bigger **family**. Then each **family** is part of a higher **order**, each **order** part of a **class**, each **class** part of a **phylum**, and each **phylum** part of a **kingdom**.

32

Each **kingdom** has thirty or more **phylums** (or, more properly, **phyla**), and each **phylum** typically contains several **classes** and **orders**, hundreds of **families** and **genuses** (or **genera**) and thousands of **species**.

Put it all together, and you have millions of species. And while we may never get round to naming them all we nonetheless have a system in place for doing it. This system is called **taxonomy**, and these naming groups are called **taxonomic groups**.

Experts guess that there are probably between 5 and 30 million species on the planet.

33

So you can name anything like that? Anything at all?

Yep. Here are a few examples for you, so you can see how your pet cat (or domestic cat) compares with an African lion, and a common chimpanzee with a human being.

Taxonomic Group

Kingdom	Animalia	Animalia	Animalia	Animalia
Phylum	Chordata	Chordata	Chordata	Chordata
Class	Mammalia	Mammalia	Mammalia	Mammalia
Order	Carnivora	Carnivora	Primates	Primates
Family	Felidae	Felidae	Hominidae	Hominidae
Genus	Felis	Panthera	Pan	Homo
Species	catus	leo	troglodytes	sapiens
Common name	cat	lion	chimp	human

Wait a minute – most of those groups are the same, aren't they?

That's right, they are. And that just shows you how closely related these animals are.

To sum up:

- All four are **Animalia** (animals), **Chordata** (things with backbones or spinal cords) and **Mammalia** (hairy things which make milk, otherwise known as mammals).

- Then you get a two-way split, as the cat and lion are both **Carnivora** (meat-eaters) and **Felidae** (cats), while the chimp and human are both **Primates** (large-brained tree-climbers with thumbs) and **Hominidae** (large, tailless apes which use their hands for gathering food, and sometimes use tools).

- Only when you get down to the level of the genus do you see them split into four totally separate groups – *Felis* (small cats), *Panthera* (big cats or panthers), *Pan* (chimpanzees) and *Homo* (humans or human-like apes).

How different would two animals have to be before they're in different classes, then?

To see a difference in **class**, you'd have to compare one of these mammals with a crocodile (class **Reptilia**), bird (class **Aves**) or newt (class **Amphibia**). For a different **phylum**, you'd need something without a backbone or spinal cord, like a wasp (phylum **Arthropoda**) or jellyfish (phylum **Cnidaria**). And for a different **kingdom**, you'd need a plant, fungus, protist or bacterium.

DIY Zoology

Have a go at classifying the animals below, by putting them in the groups that fit all their features.

Place the number corresponding to each of the following animal species into the correct area of the diagram opposite. The first one has been done for you.

1 Snow leopard (*Uncia uncia*)
2 Human (*Homo sapiens*)
3 Common chimpanzee (*Pan troglodytes*)
4 New England lobster (*Homarus americanus*)
5 Polar bear (*Ursus maritimus*)
6 African bullfrog (*Pyxicephalus adspersu*)
7 Grey squirrel (*Sciurus carolinensis*)
8 Red-tailed bumblebee (*Bombus ternaries*)
9 Black rat (*Rattus rattus*)
10 Tyrannosaurus rex

How are you supposed to remember all this stuff?

The good news is that you don't have to. Knowing some of these groupings can be handy for recognizing animals and other living things. And this, in turn, can help you see how one group might have evolved into another. But knowing every name is not that important, unless you want to be a zoologist or taxonomist.

But if you want to learn a bit about animal life — and impress your friends next time you go to the zoo — the best way is to give it a go (see below).

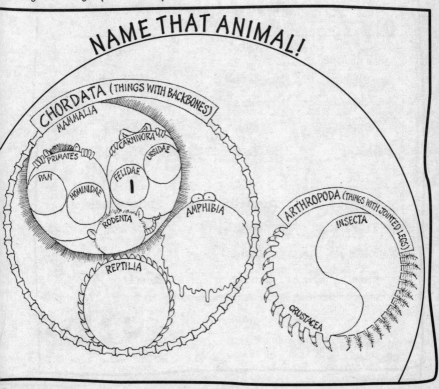

NAME THAT ANIMAL!

CHORDATA (THINGS WITH BACKBONES)
MAMMALIA
PRIMATES
CARNIVORA
PAN
FELIDAE
URSIDAE
HOMINIDAE
RODENTA
AMPHIBIA
REPTILIA
ARTHROPODA (THINGS WITH JOINTED LEGS)
INSECTA
CRUSTACEA

(answers on page 162)

Spot the Hybrid

Animals of different species can occasionally mix and mate. Sometimes they can produce healthy babies, and very occasionally this can result in the creation of a new species. But unfortunately, with some exceptions, the genes from different species generally don't mix too well, which leaves them unable to have healthy offspring.

Some of the animals below are real hybrids, made by matings between animals of different species. Others, I just made up for a laugh. Can you tell which is which?

In the wild most animals stick to mating with their own species. In captivity some animals, for example lions and tigers, will interbreed.

Snail	+	Slug	=	Snug
Hawk	+	Squirrel	=	Squawk
Lion	+	Tiger	=	Liger
Jaguar	+	Lion	=	Jaglion
Grouse	+	Owl	=	Growl
Yak	+	Cow	=	Yakow
Scorpion	+	Bumblebee	=	Scumblebee
Zebra	+	Horse	=	Zorse
Donkey	+	Zebra	=	Zeedonk
Bunny	+	Hamster	=	Bumster

(answers on page 162)

If all living things are related, does that mean my great-great-grandad was a worm?

Not quite. The great 'tree of life' does connect every living thing in the world — all the way down to fish, worms, sponges and bacteria. But different families of animal lie on different branches of the tree. So while we share ancestors and relatives with chimps, mice — even worms and jellyfish — we didn't evolve directly from the ones you see around you today.

Hold on — so all animals, including humans, are related?

Right.

... and before we were human, we were more like chimps, right?

Right. And before that, we were more like lemurs. And before *that*, more like shrews.

Okay, so my great-great-grandad was a shrew, then.

Well, I'm pretty sure your great-great-grandad was human . . .

Oh, you know what I mean. Further back than him. Like, my great-great-great-great-great . . .

Okay, okay, I get it. Go back far enough, and you will find non-human ancestors in your family tree. In fact, you only have to go back 5,000 generations (or about 100,000 years) before you reach our most recent

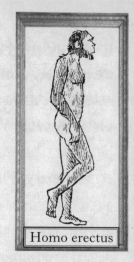

Homo erectus

non-human ancestors — the human-like (or **hominid**) ape-men known as *Homo erectus*. But you have to go back another 6 or 7 million years before you come across the ancestor we share

chimpanzee-like ape

with modern chimpanzees. (To name that ancestor, you'd have to add 300,000 'greats' to your 'grandad', and it would take you around an hour and a half to say it in full!)

To reach your most recent shrew-like ancestor, you'd have to go back 140 million years to the time of the early dinosaurs. You'd have to add so many 'great-greats' to that grandad that it would take you almost three months, speaking non-stop, to say his name.

Henkelotherium

But here's the thing, neither your chimp-like ancestor nor your mouse-like ancestor were *actually* chimps or shrews. Just as we have evolved over the millions of years since the time of those ancestors, so have modern chimps and mice. So, while it's correct to say that we have *chimp-like* or *rodent-like* ancestors, it's not true – as many people believe – that our ancestors were chimps and shrews.

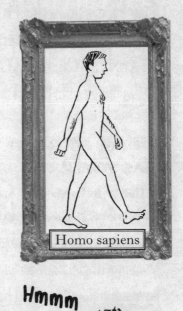

Homo sapiens

Not sure I get that.

Hmmm

It can all get a bit confusing. But that's where all that grouping and classification stuff we looked at earlier comes in really handy. Grouping animals together into families, classes and (ultimately) kingdoms allows us to talk about whole groups or related animals at once. So while we can't say your great-great-(insert 7-million more 'greats' here)-grandfather was a mouse . . . we can say that he was a rodent-like mammal, similar in appearance to a modern mouse.

In fact, this rodent-like ancestor – known as *Henkelotherium* – looked more like a tiny (7 cm-long) weasel, and had more in common with **marsupial mice** and **rats** found today in Australia and New Guinea. It may even have kept its young in a pouch, like a kangaroo!

So my ancestor was really a micro-weasel? Cool! So what came before that?

Another 140 million years before the time of *Henkelotherium*, we have animal ancestors that were reptiles. And over 100 million years earlier than those, amphibians and bony fish.

bony fish

And before that?

Before fish, there were ancestors that looked like modern

sea squirts

tunicates, also known as 'sea squirts'. These are fleshy, tubular animals that spend most of their lives stuck to a sea bed. But during their young larval stage they swim like sea worms, stiffened with a primitive type of spine (called a **notochord**). Before that, our ancestors were aquatic, wormlike creatures — little more than a head, bum and gut-tube surrounded by squishy muscle. And

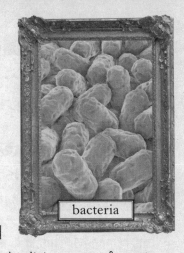

bacteria

before that: sponge-like blobs, living mats of yeast-like goo and lonely, single-celled bacteria.

So my great-great-grandad wasn't really a worm, but I do have worm-like things in my family tree?

Exactly.

And the further back in time you go, the hairier, fishier and slimier our ancestors get, right?

Er . . . I suppose you could say that, yes.

That makes sense.

Why do you say that?

Well, my grandad has hairy ears . . .

Yes, but that's not because—

. . . and sometimes his breath smells of fish . . .

Hang on, that's not very—

. . . and when he takes his false teeth out there's this slimy stuff . . .

All right, all right — enough! I get the picture.

But remember this: if it wasn't for your grandad — and for all the hairy, fishy, slimy animal ancestors that came before him — you wouldn't be here at all. So be nice.

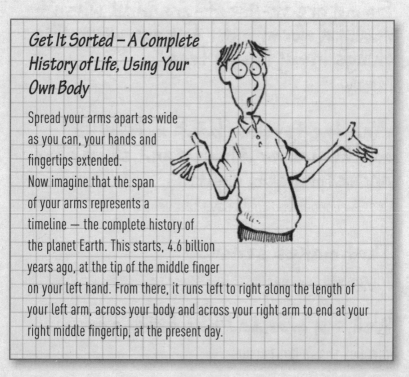

Get It Sorted – A Complete History of Life, Using Your Own Body

Spread your arms apart as wide as you can, your hands and fingertips extended. Now imagine that the span of your arms represents a timeline — the complete history of the planet Earth. This starts, 4.6 billion years ago, at the tip of the middle finger on your left hand. From there, it runs left to right along the length of your left arm, across your body and across your right arm to end at your right middle fingertip, at the present day.

- From your left middle fingertip to your left elbow is about a billion years. For that time, there was nothing but rocks and chemicals on Earth.

- From your left elbow (3.6 billion years ago), right across to your right elbow (about a billion years ago), there was nothing but single-celled bacteria and protists.

- Between your right elbow to the base of your right palm, multicellular life forms (like sponges) began to appear.

- Between the base of your palm (600 million years ago) to the base of your fingers (200 million years ago), primitive marine organisms like jellyfish and corals evolved into complex arthropods, fish, amphibians and reptiles — including, eventually, the dinosaurs.

- The dinosaurs reigned the Earth for the entire period from the base to the last knuckle of your middle finger (around 50 million years ago).

- From there to the tip of your fingernail, mammals evolved from tiny weasel-like creatures into higher mammals, including great apes and early humans.

- The entire history of the human race — from our caveman ancestors, through ancient Greece and Rome, the Dark Ages, the Middle Ages, the European colonization of America and the New World, the Napoleonic Wars, the two World Wars, the Space Age, the Internet Age and the new millennium . . . all of it could be removed with the single stroke of a file, across the tip of your right fingernail.

Kind of makes you think, doesn't it?

Why are animals all different shapes and sizes?

Because they've been mutating and evolving for millions of years – slowly adapting to fit every possible environment, diet and way of life. All the different animal shapes have come about through changes in genes and DNA – some big, some small – plus a whole lot of natural selection.

Mutating animals? You're telling me there are mutant animals all over the planet?

Yes. Absolutely.

Yaaaaaaaaaaaagh! Run for your life!

Whoa, there – easy, tiger! What's all the panic about?

Are you crazy? Mutant animals! I've seen 'em in the movies and in video games. They're all twisted and mangled, and they eat people, and . . .

Actually, outside of movies and video games, these kinds of mutants don't really even exist – so don't worry about them too much, either.

Hang on – not those kinds of mutants. I just meant animals that had mutated – or changed – from one generation to the next, through natural processes.

Oh. So . . . not . . . mutated by mad scientists with chemicals and radiation and stuff?

Er . . . no. Just natural changes in their genes (or DNA) that happen all the time, all by themselves.

Phew. That's a relief. Okay – on you go, then.

Thank you. Now where was I?

As I was saying, evolution is really all about mutating genes. This is something even Darwin didn't know. But genes are at the root of all natural selection, and they're the reason why animals (and all other living things) end up looking different from each other.

Darwin didn't know that? I thought he had evolution sussed?

Not all of it. Darwin knew that animals naturally changed from one generation to another. And he also knew that they pass these changes (or mutations) to their offspring. But he didn't know how or why they mutated, nor how the changes were passed on.

In fact, this has happened fairly recently. After factories were built in northern England in the late 1880s, the majority of the local peppered moth population shifted from speckly brown-and-white to almost black. It turned out that the darker ones were camouflaged better on the newly soot-blackened tree trunks. Now, with less pollution from factories, the populations are shifting back to their original, lighter colour.

Not being able to explain this made it difficult for him to defend his theory of relationships and evolution between animal groups. It's easy, perhaps, to imagine the gradual change of a moth's wings from brown to black ... and it's almost as easy to imagine a moth mutating into a butterfly, a bee into a wasp, even a wolf into a dog. But the jump between lobsters and llamas, jellyfish and elephants, prawns and people ... that takes some getting your head around.

Hmmm . . . I see what you mean. So how do you get from a prawn to a person? I mean, they're totally different, aren't they?

The answer lies in their DNA, in their genes.

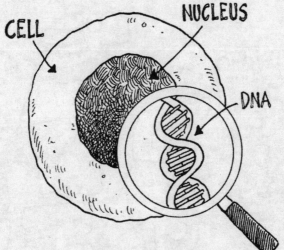

CELL

NUCLEUS

DNA

All living things contain DNA – it's in every living cell in everybody (and everybody's body!). DNA is arranged into genes – instructions that tell each growing cell (and ultimately the whole animal) how to build itself. Now, the DNA in a cell copies itself every time a cell divides. But it doesn't do it perfectly. It makes mistakes, which causes changes (or mutations) in the genes. When this happens, a number of cells may receive the wrong building instructions, causing changes (or mutations) in the animal's body.

Like an extra arm or leg?

Usually, it's not as drastic as that. Sometimes mutations do nothing, sometimes they cause big changes. It depends on the gene, and the type of mutation.

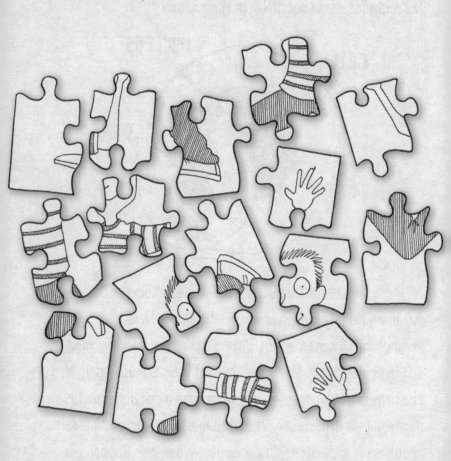

Now, one set of genes in particular — called master control genes — pretty much spell out the instructions for an animal's entire body plan. They tell the growing embryo where to put the head and tail end, how many arms, legs or wings it should have (and where they should go), how the guts, bones and nerves develop . . . the works. If these genes mutate, the animal's body plan can be changed enormously.

For example, one set of genes decides which side of the body the spine and the guts will end up on. In humans and other vertebrates, the backbone — of course — goes at the back, while the guts run down the ventral (or belly) side of the body. But in prawns, lobsters, spiders and other **arthropods**, it's the other way around. These animals don't have backbones, of course. But they do have primitive spinal cords (or notochords) that run through their bellies, while their guts run along their backs. If you've ever eaten prawns, you may have noticed this. Sometimes, you find a little 'vein' running down their backs, right? Well, that's actually their gut (which is why it's best to cut this out before eating them — who wants to eat prawn poo?), sitting where the spine would be in a reptile or mammal.

So how did that happen?

This happened because at some point in the past the animal that eventually evolved into prawn had its body plan flipped upside down, because — and this is the important bit — two of its master genes were mutated. So all at once you've had a fork in the road. One led to a group of animals

(fish, amphibians, reptiles, birds and mammals) with backbones in their backs and guts in their bellies, while the other led to animals (prawns, lobsters, spiders and other arthropods) with guts in their backs instead.

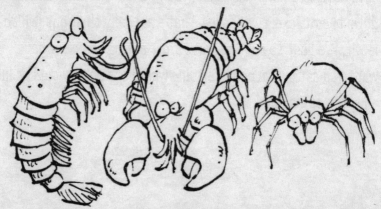

So in a way people are like upside-down prawns?

Exactly! And it's changes like this that have led to the huge variety of animal body plans that you see around you today. Everything from a bell-shaped jellyfish to a tubular eel. From a four-legged hippo to a two-legged human.

Wow. Giant tube-fish and two-legged, mutant prawn-people. They should make a video game out of that. Or a movie at the very least . . .

Fit for Battle

Evolution is all about 'survival of the fittest', but there are lots of ways for an animal to be 'fit' or well suited to their environment. Instead of a race or competition, think of it like a war. In a real battle, it's not always the biggest, strongest or fastest soldiers that win the fight. It's often the soldiers with the better weapons, technology and tactics.

Camouflage

Tigers, polar bears and other mammals turn themselves into 'stealth fighters' by blending into their backgrounds with their coat colours. Caterpillars and stick insects imitate twigs and leaves to hide from birds, and sloths hang in the trees looking like a mossy bunch of branches. Chameleons and cuttlefish have adaptive camouflage that can change colour in minutes or even seconds. In fact, the whole idea of military camouflage came from animals in the first place.

Blades

Most cats, dogs, bears and other carnivores have sharp, blade-like canine teeth in their mouths, and a handful of sharp blades on each paw. Mess with those bad boys at your peril.

Body-armour

Animals like tortoises and armadillos evolved thick armour plating to protect themselves.

The pangolin – a type of tree-dwelling anteater found in Africa and Asia – has even evolved a coat of spectacular, overlapping scales, giving it flexible armour plating that would be the envy of any medieval knight or samurai.

Firepower

Archerfish can shoot dragonflies off twigs with high-pressure streams of water, often with incredible accuracy. Jellyfish and anemones fire poison-filled harpoons into their victims.

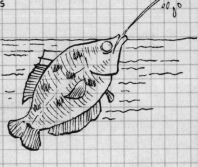

Chemical weapons

Skunks deter predators with a foul-smelling urine spray. And many snakes, spiders and other venomous animals can paralyse or kill with their deadly, toothy poisons.

Technology

Radar and sonar were first seen in the animal world. Dolphins and cave swifts use rapid clicking sounds to locate each other and their prey. Bats, famously, can use waves of ultrasound to hunt moths in complete darkness. In response, some moths have joined the arms race by fighting back, using sonar-jamming screams.

Team-tactics

Think of a pride of lionesses stalking antelopes, or a wolf pack circling deer in a forest, to see team-tactics in action. Dolphins work together to chase fish and chimps manoeuvre small monkeys into traps and ambushes. Many ants, termites and other insects form entire armies, working together to find food or fight off attackers.

My mum said yesterday that my goldfish needs a new tank. Maybe they're getting ready for an attack. I'm not sure they'll know how to drive it, though...

Secret Weapon

Match each animal with its own secret weapon for survival.

hyena   body armour

ibex   teeth

warthog   camouflage

tiger   antlers

bat   deadly venom

cobra   tusks

skunk   ultrasound

pangolin   chemical spray

leaf mantis   claws

(answers on page 163)

THE SPINELESS CREW

Why are trees and plants all green, but mushrooms are white, brown or red?

Because mushrooms are not plants. Nor are they even especially related to plants. They sit in their own kingdom of life – **fungi** – and are actually closer cousins to us animals!

What? Oh, come off it. You don't expect me to believe that.

Believe what?

That mushrooms are animals. I mean, when was the last time

a mushroom ate anyone? Do they creep around the forest stalking mice and rabbits while we're not looking? Don't be daft. This is a wind-up.

It's not. Honest! Although they share some features with both, fungi *really* are more closely related to animals than they are plants. It's true that — like trees and flowers — they tend to stay put throughout their lifetimes. But it's what they do while they sit there that makes them so different to plants . . . and more similar to primitive animals.

What's that, then?

In short, they're scoffers, not growers. Consumers, rather than producers. They get their food and energy in a very different way.

Plants basically feed themselves. They use a green-coloured chemical called **chlorophyll** to trap energy from sunlight. Then they use that energy to convert water and carbon dioxide gas, from the soil and air around them, into sugars and oxygen. Then they eat the sugars and release the oxygen. Which is very nice of them, because without this process — known as **photosynthesis** (or 'light-building'), we wouldn't have any oxygen to breathe.

So how are mushrooms any different?

Mushrooms, toadstools and other types of fungi don't photosynthesize. At all. Like animals, they're *heterotrophs* (or 'other-eaters'). They eat the sugars thoughtfully provided by plants and other self-feeding things.

But why can't they just feed themselves, like plants?

They didn't evolve to. Unlike plants, they can't photosynthesize — because they lack the green chlorophyll chemical they'd need to do it. (This is also, incidentally, why fungi are usually not green, as almost all plants are.) So, instead, fungi feed on plant and animal wastes, or upon their dead, decomposing bodies.

Ugh!

They eat rotten, dead bodies and poo?

Very often, yes. (Bet you won't look at the mushrooms on your fry-up quite the same way again, eh?) But most often mushrooms feed on leaf litter around tree roots, or attach themselves to still-living trees and plants themselves in order to feed on its waste products.

Doesn't that hurt the tree?

Sometimes, yes. Some fungi are parasites which damage or kill the plants they grow on. But others form a kind of friendly partnership, called a symbiosis. Some fungi attach themselves to plant roots and extend finger-like threads into the surrounding soil to absorb water and nutrients.

Farmers and gardeners spend billions of pounds every year on anti-fungal sprays and soil additives.

60

The fungus then passes these to the growing plant, which returns the favour by supplying it with sugary food and minerals.

Okay, so fungi look like plants, but behave more like animals?

Right. Like dolphins and monkeys, plants and fungi share a common ancestor, but they're not the same thing at all. And just as monkeys are more closely related to humans than dolphins, studies of plant and fungal DNA have revealed that fungi are closer to animals than they are to plants.

Which, to me, comes as no surprise.

Why's that?

I've always thought of myself as a pretty fun guy. Fun-guy. Fungi. Geddit?

That was awful.

Sorry. I guess there's not mush-room in this book for gags like that.

Groan.

Hehehehheh.

Animal Magic

Is there an animal that multiplies when it's chopped into bits?

Yes! While it is rare, at least two types of animal can do this. The vast majority of animals die if you chop them up. But many reptiles, amphibians, spiders and insects can survive having large bits chopped off their bodies.

And among the simpler animal families, some are almost indestructible through choppage!

So if you chop a lizard in two, you get two lizards?

Er ... no, you definitely don't. Some lizards can survive losing limbs (though they don't enjoy it, so please don't go around testing this). And some think so little of losing their tails that they'll happily allow a predator to rip them off in order to escape being eaten. But you don't get two lizards. Just one very relieved lizard and the dead limb or tail it leaves behind.

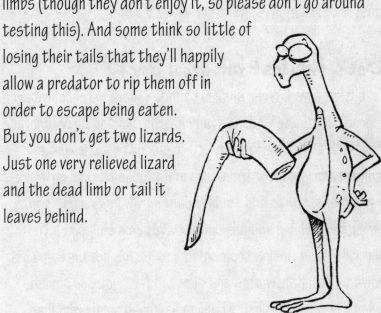

Happily, most lizard species that do this also regenerate their tails again afterwards! Although presumably they don't much enjoy this, since the new tail is usually a bit stumpier, and they can only do this a few times before they end up totally tail-less.

What about snakes?

Despite what you may have heard, snakes will die if you chop them in half, not go on to live in two halves. Depending on where you chop them, some snakes can survive losing a good chunk (up to half the length of) their bodies. But both halves don't live – one (the bit with the head end, with its neural cluster of brain) lives, while the other bit dies.

Does the lost bit grow back?

Sometimes, yes. While snakes cannot generally regenerate (or regrow) lost body lengths, many lizards can and do regenerate limbs and tails from limb buds – in much the same way as animal embryos grow arms, legs and tails in the egg or womb. Some frogs, newts and spiders can regrow body parts too. But none of these animals can survive being chopped into several bits, or losing their entire heads. It's not until you get down to starfish, worms and sponges that you see animals able to regenerate their whole bodies from single remaining pieces.

Why is that?

It's all to do with brains. Complex animals like mammals, reptiles, amphibians and insects have large clusters of nerves (or neural tissue) in their heads, which we call brains. Even in the humble lizard or spider, the brain controls essential functions like breathing and blood circulation. Unlike bone and muscle, the brain is very hard to do without, and even harder to replace. Even for very talented reptilian regenerators that regrow lost tissues very quickly, it simply can't be regrown before the rest of the animal's body dies — through lack of blood supply and oxygen.

So how do worms, starfish and sponges do it?

Partly by having even greater powers of regeneration, but also by being less dependent on brains. Worms and starfish don't have brains as such — just small nerve clusters that control bodily functions in much simpler ways. If you cut an arm off a starfish — provided there's still a good chunk of the middle bit (containing the neural cluster) left attached to it — then an entire starfish can sometimes regenerate from that single limb.

Wow! Cool!

But once again — please don't go to the beach and try this. They really don't enjoy it, and many starfish species will simply die instead. So just take my word for it.

Okay. So how what about worms?

Worms can go one better. Having an even simpler body plan, many types of flatworm can regenerate from any detached body part — head, tail or middle — as long as some neural tissue remains. Planaria flatworms can be sliced in half crosswise or lengthwise, and each half will regenerate into a complete worm. Some can even be cut into several bits, with each one regrowing to form a complete living worm.

This would be us losing all four limbs and a head, and regrowing it all from the spinal cord outwards.

Whoa! Freaky!

Sponges, however, probably take the prize. Sponges are the simplest animals in existence — they're basically little more than clusters of intercommunicating cells, formed around a sandy or chalky skeleton. Their bodies can be shapeless blobs, or simple tubes. They absorb nutrients and oxygen from the water around them, and transport it around the body using pumps and channels between the communicating cells.

But the animal never moves. It just sits there for life on the seabed. Until, that is, it reproduces. Then it buds off little swimming spongelets (like little sperm), which swim off to fertilize egg cells released by other sponges, and settles down on a new spot of seabed to grow into a new animal.

But here's the cool thing: you can take a sponge, put it in a blender, shove the bits through a filter and leave them in a tube or tank, and guess what happens! Yep — the sponge will spontaneously reassemble itself like some sort of indestructible alien zombie!

Cool! So could we ever learn to do that?

Unfortunately, humans could never survive the 'blender treatment', since our bodies are way too specialized. Even worms are too complex for that one. But scientists are studying starfish, salamanders and other regenerating animals in an effort to find out how they regrow muscle, bone and nerve tissue. It's hoped that one day, we might figure out exactly how they do it, and create drugs to trigger ancient genes, lying deep within our DNA, that cause damaged limbs, organs and brains to repair themselves through regeneration.

That would be brilliant!

Indeed. But until they do figure it out I'd avoid doing anything that might result in lost limbs. Like playing with samurai swords. Or jumping into blenders.

Jellyfish . . . and Other Unusual Animals

Do sharks eat jellyfish for dessert?

No, they don't. While some turtles eat jellyfish, sharks and other fish tend to avoid them, as eating one feels much like munching down a slimy stinging-nettle salad.

Ouch. That doesn't sound too tasty. Not a bit like jelly and ice cream.

Not at all. Unfortunately for sharks, jellyfish don't come in lime and strawberry flavours. Come to think of it, even if they did, it's still not clear whether sharks would dig them. They'd probably prefer seal flavour, or perhaps surfer's leg flavour. In any case, jellyfish taste pretty horrible (I ate one once in Japan – bleurgh). And, worse still, unless they're carefully dispatched and prepared by a cunning chef, most jellyfish mount some pretty vicious defences to avoid being eaten.

Ha Ha! Joke! While they do like seals, sharks don't really like the taste of surfers. They usually just bite them by mistake, thinking they're seals or turtles. There's another book by Glenn, 'Stuff That Scares Your Pants Off!', with more about shark attacks and surfers.

You mean the stingers?

Right. Or, rather, the stinging cells. Jellyfish belong to a class of animals called *Cnidaria* — the word comes from the Greek for 'nettles'. (See? They really are like living nettle salads!) All Cnidaria carry thousands of specialized stinging cells (or cnidocytes), usually on the surface of their flailing tentacles. Inside each one is a tiny, microscopic, poison-filled harpoon.

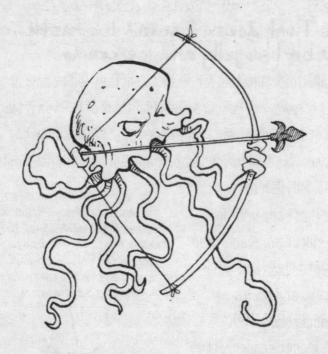

Touching a tentacle (even just barely brushing it) is enough to trigger the weapon. With incredible speed, the harpoon explodes out of the cell like a high-pressure, water-powered rocket. Once inside the target, it wedges itself within the flesh with arrow-like, backwards-facing barbs, and releases its poison into the surrounding tissues and bloodstream. Using these micro-harpoons, a cnidarian can paralyse or kill insects, fish and – occasionally – people. Some turtles, however, have become immune to the stingers. Which is why they – and only they – bother to eat them.

Blimey. That all sounds a bit clever. I didn't think jellyfish were that smart. I thought they were just brainless, drifting blobs in the sea

Well, in a way they are. Jellyfish and other cnidarians lack anything approaching a real brain. And most are content to drift in ocean currents to find prey and mates – doing little more than controlling their depth with their squidgy, rippling muscle contractions. But for many reasons they're also unique and fascinating animals. A glimpse of our evolutionary past.

How's that, then?

For starters, many cnidarians (not only jellyfish, but also **sea anemones**, **corals** and freshwater **hydras**) are **polymorphs**, or shape-shifters. Their bodies can take one of two major shapes, and they shift between them at different stages of their lives.

The first shape is called a polyp form, which looks a bit like a flower or upturned sink plunger. Anemones and corals remain in this shape throughout their entire adult lives, stuck upside-down to rocks or seabeds with their stinging tentacles waving in the water. When they reproduce, bits of themselves bud off from the main body and float to another site.

In some species, these baby anenomes and corals stay in the polyp form. But in others they shift to the second shape — the medusa form. This looks much like you'd imagine a jellyfish — like a see-through umbrella without a handle. The medusa form then swims about breeding with others, until it eventually lays a fertilized egg, which in turn becomes another anemone or coral polyp.

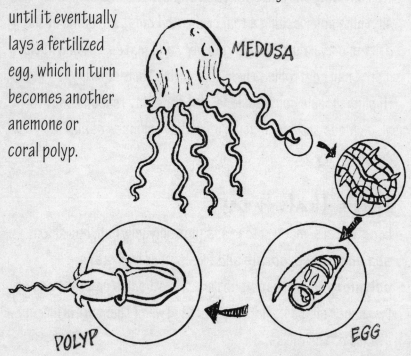

MEDUSA

EGG

POLYP

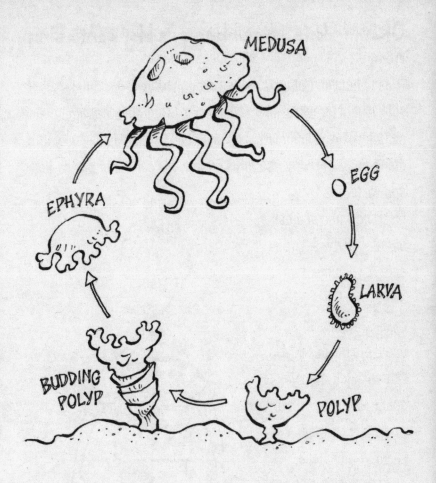

MEDUSA

EGG

EPHYRA

LARVA

BUDDING
POLYP

POLYP

Jellyfish, on the other hand, do things the other way round.
They spend their entire adult lives in the umbrella shape, then
lay eggs which develop into tiny baby polyps. These stay on
the seabed until mature, at which point they bud off into a
medusa form, which grows into an adult jellyfish.

Okay – this is getting pretty confusing now . . .

It gets better. Cnidarians are among the very few animals with radial (or wheel-like) symmetry. Most animals (humans included) are symmetrical on one side-to-side axis – so you could put a mirror vertically through the centre of our bodies, and we look more or less the same on both sides. Two eyes, two ears, two lungs, two arms, two legs . . . each pair the same basic shape and size. But with jellyfish you could place the mirror vertically through them at any angle, and they will look the same on either side of it – like a wheel or a big round birthday cake.

This is also why they lack a single, solid brain. Since they look the same from all sides, they could encounter food or predators from any side. So there's no point in developing a 'head' end with a brain. Instead, they have rings of nerves that encircle their umbrella-like bodies, forming a **neural net** for basic control over its body systems.

Swimming, poisonous birthday cakes. Weird.

Finally – just to top off the weirdness – jellyfish and anemones also lack guts. So they eat and poo through the same hole. **Ugh!**

Seriously?

Seriously. Anything unlucky enough to drift into their mouths, or into the space beneath their umbrella-like mantles, gets digested and pulled into the tubular oral lobe sticking up (or hanging down) through the centre. Any undigested bits are then spewed (or pooed, depending on how you look at it) back through the same opening.

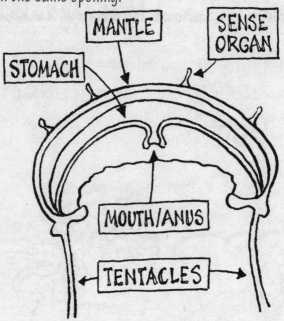

Gross! So could a jellyfish eat a person?

No. Fortunately, they don't grow big (or hungry) enough to do this. And although a few cnidarians (like fire corals, box jellyfish and sea wasps) can be harmful to swimmers and divers, most are just a nuisance. Which is fortunate, since jellyfish numbers have been steadily increasing as sea temperatures gradually rise under the influence of global warming. Already, some swimming beaches in Europe and Australia are being closed every year due to annual jellyfish swarms.

No problem – I've got a plan to deal with that.

What's that, then?

Just swim behind a hungry turtle!

Get It Sorted – Facts About Cnidaria

A few species of jellyfish, such as the box jellyfish, the sea wasp and the Portuguese man-of-war, have stings powerful enough to harm humans. Box jelly stings are so painful they can send victims into spontaneous heart attacks.

Clownfish — made famous by the movie *Finding Nemo* — are immune to anemone stings, and make nests among their stinging tentacles to stay safe from bigger fish.

Hermit crabs go one better — they often place anenomes on their shells on purpose, creating weaponized, mobile fortresses to ward off fish and octopus attacks!

Amazing Insects
Why are there no car-sized bugs and beetles?

Because of the way their bodies are built. Bugs and beetles are like knights in thick armour. Their heavy outer skeletons are great for protection, but if they're built too big they're too heavy to move.

But insects don't seem very heavy. I mean, you can hardly feel them when they walk on you.

That's because they're usually pretty tiny. But if you think about their larger cousins, crabs and lobsters, you start to get an idea of how heavy a big bug would be.

Crabs, lobsters, spiders, scorpions and insects form part of a larger group of animals called **arthropods**.

'Arthro-pod' literally means 'jointed legs', which describes their knight-in-armour-style body shapes. Arthropods are basically like us, inside out. Instead of having solid bones surrounded by pulling muscles, they have their skeleton on the outside and muscles on the inside. Their exoskeletons are made of a tough protein called chitin, which forms a solid shell around their bodies and hard tubes around their limbs.

But if they're all rigid and stiff, then how do they move at all?

Ahhh, that's where the joints come in. The stiff shells and tubes are jointed, and the muscles that move their bodies are attached to the insides of them. This gives them rigid bodies, but flexible, movable legs. The arthropod's body is built in sections or **segments**, and pairs of limbs stick out from the side or the bottom of certain body segments. The typical insect, like an ant or beetle, has a head, thorax and abdomen, along with three pairs of leg segments, giving them six legs altogether. To move, each leg moves (from the 'hip' joint where it contacts the body) up, forward, back, then down in an alternating pattern, driving the insect forward.

HEAD

THORAX

ABDOMEN

FEMUR

TIBIA

TARSUS

For the small insects, this works very well. The hollow, shell-like armour protects them from predators, and they stay mobile. But beyond a certain size, these tubes and shells would buckle under their own weight, leaving them paralysed and vulnerable to attack. That's why insects typically don't get bigger than a few centimetres or inches across. The largest beetles and bugs in the world live in South America and China, and even they rarely reach over 18 cm (7 inches) long. Big enough to be scary, perhaps, but certainly not man-eaters.

Get It Sorted – Arachnids and Myriapods

Arachnids

Spiders and scorpions are arachnids and have different body shapes and lifestyles. They also have four pairs of legs rather than three, and use different hunting tactics that don't require so much movement — such as lying in wait on a web and paralysing their prey with stings. Still, the largest spiders and scorpions grow no more than 30 cm (12 inches) across.

Myriapods

Millipedes and centipedes are in the myriapod (meaning 'many legs') family, and some use their extra legs to support their extra size and weight. African giant millipedes can grow up to 38 cm (15 inches) long.

The largest arthropods around are the aquatic ones – the crustaceans. Crabs and lobsters have five pairs of legs (ten altogether), and rely on buoyancy from the water to help support their heavy bodies, so they can grow much larger. North Atlantic lobsters reach up to **60 cm (2 feet)**, while Japanese spider crabs have bodies over 30 cm across, and a leg span of up to **6 metres (20 feet)**!

Now you're talking! That's massive!

Of course, not all insects trot along the ground or seabed. Some have, very successfully, taken to the air – like flies, beetles, bees, wasps and butterflies. But again there's a limit to how huge they can grow.

Small insects like bees and wasps fly by beating their wings very rapidly and creating swelling vortices in the air, which help keep them aloft, but then flying is more like swimming through a gloopy

liquid than gliding or flapping through thin air. The bigger you get the harder you fall. Or, rather, the harder it is to stay airborne. This is why flying insects no longer get very big at all.

The largest wasp in the world, the Tarantula Hawk Wasp, is only **12 cm (5 inches)** long, while the largest living flying insect – the Chinese giant water-bug – has a wingspan of around **20 cm (8 inches)**. Which, admittedly, you'd need a cricket bat to swat. But it's still pretty harmless, and not quite in pterodactyl territory.

Tarantula Hawk Wasps live in South America and actually attack and kill tarantulas. They get all the crazy bugs down there.

What do you mean 'no longer' get very big?

Well, at other times in the Earth's history, some bugs, such as dragonflies, were quite a bit bigger. This was because the atmosphere was warmer and thicker, providing more lift and oxygen for energetic, big-bug flight. Some prehistoric dragonflies reached sizes of up to 70 cm (4 feet) across.

Now that's a big bug.

Odd Bug Out

Spot the odd one out in each group of four animals below.

1. stag   fruit   butterfly   millipede
    beetle   fly

2. daddy   tarantula   camel   deer tick
    long-legs   spider

3. hermit   cuttlefish   prawn   lobster
    crab

4. dragonfly   spider   starfish   barnacle
                 crab

(answers on page 163)

Slime Central!

Why are slugs and snails so slimy?

For three main reasons. First, it keeps them from drying out in dry air. Second, it allows them to climb and crawl upside down. And, third, it makes them taste revolting.

But why would they have to worry about drying out?

Because they evolved in water and adapted to live in air.

Some molluscs – like limpets – can survive for hours in the open air, between tides, by clamping their shells tightly to rocks. But slugs and snails are the only molluscs that can survive out of the water indefinitely.

You have to remember that slugs, snails and other **molluscs** first evolved to live in the sea. Most of them – like clams, mussels, limpets, cuttlefish, squid and octopus – simply stayed there.

But slugs and snails alone left the water for the air, and when they did they had to find a way of keeping their bodies moist in the dry air around them.

Part of the solution to this was to secrete a slimy layer of mucus from glands in their skin. This layer then forms a waterproof barrier that prevents water from evaporating out of their bodies.

Get It Sorted – Worm Slime

Worms, who also first evolved in the sea, had to find a way of both staying moist and getting oxygen from the air around them * once they moved out of the water and into the open air.

So, they secrete a layer of slimy mucus from their skin, which, like snails, prevents water from evaporating out, but also allows oxygen to dissolve into their bodies. Yep, they breathe through their skin, a bit like turning your lungs inside out, and wearing them like a wetsuit.

In this way worms can not only survive underwater and underground, but also deep inside animal bodies – beneath skin, and inside blood vessels and organs.

* In the sea the oxygen from the water around them could simply drift (or diffuse) through their bodies.

And also makes them slimy and gross, right?

Right. In fact, some slugs and snails secrete a toxic (or, at the very least, very nasty-tasting) slime that discourages birds, reptiles and mammals from eating them. Although this doesn't seem to dissuade French chefs, who boil off the slime and coat them with butter and garlic instead.

Urrrghhh.

I'll never understand that.

Me neither.

So why do snails have shells, but slugs don't?

Because slugs don't really need them.

But why? Doesn't being shell-less leave slugs a bit – you know – defenceless?

Well, for land snails, shells are really more of a protection against drying out than they are against predators. They're too thin to serve as real armour, as they do in clams and mussels. On land, birds and rodents and predators usually just crunch right through the shells, or whack them against rocks until they burst open. It also takes quite a bit of time and energy to make a shell. Not to mention lots of calcium – which means snails can only live in areas with calcium-rich soils and plants.

Slugs, evidently, figured this out. So at some point they stopped making shells, and began secreting a thicker, stickier slime to replace the shell instead. Which — unless you're nasty enough to pour salt on them — protects them from drying out quite nicely.

So slugs used to have shells?

Yes. And, in fact, many of them still do! You just can't see them. Many slug species build thin shell-like layers of calcium under their skin (or mantle) — revealing their snail-like evolutionary past.

Besides that, slugs and snails have many other things in common too. They each have a rasping, toothy tongue called a *radula*, some bearing hundreds or thousands of teeth, which they use to snip and scrape at their food.

MUNCH!
MUNCH!

Snails and slugs have teeth? No way!

Yes, way. How did you think they did that much damage to lettuces and other plant leaves? By sucking on them?

Oh. Didn't think of that . . .

They also have one or two pairs of tentacles (with eyes at the base), plus a single squishy foot that they use for crawling along surfaces. And this is where their slime really comes into its own.

How's that?

The slime works as both an oily lubricant, and a sticky glue.

It sticks the slime or snail to almost any surface, allowing it to crawl straight upward, or even upside down, using wave-like rippling motions of its foot.

But if it's glued to the surface, how does it move at all?

As the animal pushes its muscular foot forward, the glue towards the rear of the foot breaks, and the foot peels away. When the animal stops moving, the glue re-forms, holding it fast to the surface. So it sort of sticks and slides its way along, leaving a trail of goo in its wake.

Yuck! Snails are gross.

You think that's gross? Get this — somewhere along the line of snail evolution, their guts twisted through 180 degrees so that their bums now lie directly above their heads, just beneath the shell. So snails poo on their own heads.

Why would they do that? What are they, stupid or something?

To be honest, no one really knows how or why this happened. It doesn't seem to make a lot of sense, as it means they constantly risk fouling on their gills — literally breathing in their poo and choking to death on it. But somehow they seem to get by.

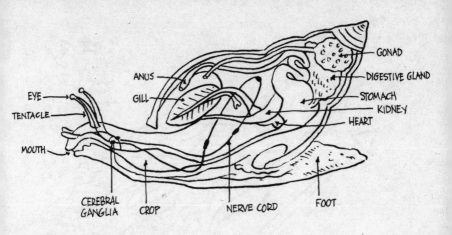

Diagram labels: GONAD, DIGESTIVE GLAND, STOMACH, KIDNEY, HEART, ANUS, GILL, EYE, TENTACLE, MOUTH, CEREBRAL GANGLIA, CROP, NERVE CORD, FOOT

So molluscs breathe through gills, then? Not lungs?

Sea snails — and most other molluscs — have gills. But in land snails these have turned into true lungs, which draw air in and out using muscles, much as ours do. Either way, the breathing organs sit just between the head and the shell, on the surface of the **mantle**. In octopus and squid, the largest members of the mollusc family, the pumping gills can also take on another function entirely: jet propulsion.

Really? I thought they just kind of squidged around using tentacles.

Octopuses do crawl on surfaces, but when startled they can also jet away at high speed by drawing water into their mantle cavities and blasting it out in the opposite direction to the

way they want to go. And squid jet about like this all the time. Perhaps thanks to this faster, jet-propelled movement, squid, cuttlefish and octopus (all in the same family, called **cephalopods**) have evolved to become agile carnivorous predators, rather than passive, slimy plant and plankton feeders. They have keen vision and reflexes, and are also very smart, as invertebrates go. Squid and cuttlefish are known to communicate with each other using light patterns strobed across their bodies, while octopuses have been shown to have a cunning problem-solving intelligence when hunting.

They also get big. Very big. Giant squid grow to over **10 m (30 feet)**, and regularly do battle with sperm whales. And the recently discovered colossal squid grows to **13 m (40 feet)** and perhaps much larger.

Freaky! So if they're so smart and deadly, why have squid and octopus never crawled out of the ocean to live on the land, and – you know – evolved into squid-people or something?

Partly because they couldn't get about too easily. Their water-filled tentacles are adapted to moving underwater, and are floppy and useless on land. (If you've ever seen a squid or octopus out of the water, you'll know what I mean.) Which is probably quite a good thing for us land animals.

What about on another planet? Could it happen there?

Who knows? I do know this – a race of air-breathing squid-people would be scary. Think about it – cephalopods are intelligent, communicative, stealthy and carnivorous. Here, they're kept in check by being unable to leave the water and, even if they did, they'd face large predators and competition on land.

Yeah! Maybe elsewhere they might evolve super-intelligence and superior technology. Then they could mount a full-on alien mollusc invasion! Then what would we do?

Send in the French, maybe. Armed with big dinner forks and blobs of garlic butter.

BIG THINGS WITH BACKBONES

Why do crocodiles wriggle when they walk?

Because – like most other reptiles – crocodiles can't rotate their hips or shoulders. So they have to wriggle their spines from side to side in order to 'snake' their way forward. Reptiles are built differently to mammals, so, while they're more agile on land than fish and amphibians, they're a poor second to cats, dogs, horses and humans when it comes to walking, running and jumping.

Why's that? I thought lizards and crocodiles could move pretty fast.

Some can, but they're not in the same league as mammals.

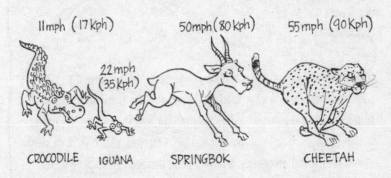

11mph (17kph)   50mph (80kph)   55mph (90kph)

22mph (35kph)

CROCODILE IGUANA   SPRINGBOK   CHEETAH

What's more, cheetahs and gazelles can dodge and turn as they do so. No reptile is capable of agility like this.

Why not?

Because of the way their bodies are built and how they have evolved. But rather than just tell you all about it let's do a little experiment . . .

Walk Like a . . . Fish?

Lie on the floor, belly down, and let your arms flop loosely at your sides. Imagine you've been bitten by a snake, and your arms and legs are paralysed. You can't feel them or move them at all. Now try moving your whole body across the floor, just using your shoulders, hips, and the wriggling of your spine.

Not too easy, is it? But this is pretty much all a **fish** can do, which allows them to swim and turn in water, but on land spine-wriggling alone isn't much cop.

Now let's try evolving into a **reptile** . . . Get on the floor once again, this time on all fours, with your hands and feet touching the ground. Now turn your feet outwards, as far as they will go, and your hands inward, so that your fingers point towards each other. Keep your chest and hips very low to the ground, imagine you have a stick threaded through your shirt from elbow to elbow, and crawl forward using alternating steps of your hands and feet.

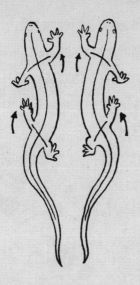

It's tricky, but a bit faster and easier than fish. This is how newts, lizards and crocodiles move – crawling, running and even (some of them) jumping. But since the shoulders and hips of most reptiles can't rotate freely and independently (as they do in mammals) they have to wriggle their whole bodies like leggy land-fish in order to move. Which tends to limit their speed and agility.

Now let's evolve into **mammals**. Go down on all fours – hands and feet – but this time, straighten out your hands and feet so that they point forward. Come up on to your toes, and hold your body a little higher off the ground. Now try moving forward once again. With a bit of practice (and imagination!) you should be able to manage a sinister, cat-like stalk (more like walking than crawling).

Many dinosaurs (and other now-extinct prehistoric reptiles) had slightly different hip structures, allowing animals like Velociraptor and Gallimimus to move terrifyingly fast.

So with freed up shoulders and hips, and knees and elbows which face each other (rather than sticking out sideways) mammals became skilled runners, jumpers, dodgers and weavers.

Cool! We mammals rule.

And, if you think about it, this is also how we learn to move as we grow from babies to toddlers to children. First, a baby learns to wriggle its spine, so that it can roll over and sit up by itself. Then it learns to crawl, and finally to walk, run and jump. Reptiles, on the other hand, stop developing their movements at the stiff, crawling stage. And though some of them can crawl pretty fast (and a few can even stand up and run), they've got nothing on us mammals.

When did fish grow feet – was it before or after they left the water?

Almost certainly before, because without them their air-breathing amphibian descendants couldn't even have got out of the water, let alone enjoyed any advantage of being on the land. In fact, not only frog feet, but also lizard limbs, mouse paws and human hands all evolved from the fleshy fins of fish.

Are you sure? Couldn't they have just jumped out of the water, and flopped around a bit first?

Okay . . . and then what would they do?

Er . . . I dunno. Snap at a passing insect, then flop their way back into the water?

Well, we've already seen how ill-equipped limbless fish are for moving on land – you tried it yourself, remember? Sharks occasionally beach themselves trying to catch seals in shallow waters, and it doesn't usually work out too well for them. Out of the water, they suffocate in minutes.

Yeah, but sharks can't breathe out of the water, can they? What if the fish evolved lungs, and then flopped on to the beach?

Well, whales can breathe out of the water, but beaching doesn't usually go too well for them, either.

Okay, fine. But what if they were smaller, lighter fish that could move themselves about on the shore?

Good point. But to actively hunt, breed or survive for any decent length of time out of the water, the fish would already need some way of lifting and shifting its body on land. Namely, muscular legs. Or, at least, the beginnings of them. And that, it turns out, is almost certainly what the earliest, fishy land-explorers had.

A few species of fish – called, unsurprisingly, lungfish – have actually evolved primitive lungs, which allow them to survive droughts by burrowing underground and going into a kind of summer hibernation.

Just a few years ago, fossil-hunting scientists found some incredible evidence of how fish first left the water to become **tetrapods** (four-legged land animals, like frogs, lizards and weasels). It was, quite literally, a fish that could do a push-up.

What? You're joking, right?

Nope. That's exactly what it was. This ancient fossil fish of the *Tiktaalik* genus lived around 375 million years ago.

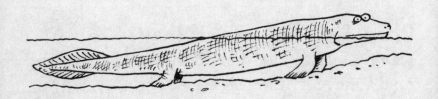

And what makes it special is that its front fins have obvious wrist bones and bony 'fingers', allowing the animal to flex them and lift itself up. While its fins probably weren't strong enough for it to walk, it could nonetheless do something like a push-up to lift its head out of the water — perhaps to catch flying insects. Experts believe that *Tiktaalik* probably evolved into something like *Acanthostega* or *Icythyostega* (swamp-dwelling animals a bit like giant salamanders, which are the earliest known tetrapods) and — eventually — dinosaurs and other land-based reptiles.

Get It Sorted — Lost Limbs

Animals can also lose features they gained through evolution. Snakes lost their legs,* as did whales and dolphins when they returned to the sea. And other animals have gained (and later lost) tails, fur, feathers . . . even eyes and ears.

It all depends on what's needed to survive, and what's not. Natural selection doesn't care what the animal looks like. Some live, some die, some breed, others fail, and in the end the best-adapted animals survive, regardless of what they may look like (or whether they quite enjoyed having legs, thank you very much).

OOPS!

* Believe it or not, some living snake species still have hip bones and leg bones tucked away beneath their scaly skin!

So the muscly foot evolved while the fish still lived underwater?

Exactly.

But why would it need a foot underwater?

Possibly to help it scoot along shallow shorelines or riverbeds, as modern manatees (which are, of course, mammals — but you get the idea) do. And once it was muscly enough to prop the fish up, new possibilities emerged — like finding new food on land, or escaping sharks and other predators in the water. So natural selection happily took care of the rest.

So evolution nicked a fin to make a foot.

Exactly! This 'nicking' of one structure (like a fin) to make another (like a foot) is actually quite common in evolution. It's far easier to adjust an old body part to a new purpose rather than develop a new one from scratch. The same applies to eyes, wings and even parts of our brains.

So, after that, fish evolved into amphibians, lizards and mammals?

That's right, they did.

The very first fish were like flattish worms with no jaws, eyes, fins or backbone. Later, they developed into eel-like fish with fleshy fins and sucking mouths, like the **hagfish** and **lampreys** we still see today. After those came fish with bony jaws and fins. It was these bony fish with backbones that later left the seas for life on land, via early fishy tetrapods (or 'fishapods') like *Tiktaalik*.

With the fishapod's backbone, spinal cord and muscly limbs came mobility, power and strength. And it was this that allowed them to spread into a wider range of successful body types – amphibians, lizards, birds, mammals and more.

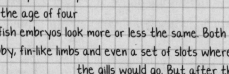

Get It Sorted – Our Fishy History!

Fish are our evolutionary ancestors, in that they were the first vertebrates, or backboned animals.

In fact, even today, you can still see evidence of this fishy ancestry in our bodies. Up to the age of four weeks, human and fish embryos look more or less the same. Both have long tails stubby, fin-like limbs and even a set of slots where the gills would go. But after that, human embryos lose their tails as the spine stops developing at the tailbone (or coccyx). Their stubby limb buds grow into arms and legs, and the ancient gill bones become part of the jaw, inner ear and larynx (or voice box).

FISH EMBRYO

HUMAN EMBRYO

Why are frogs always gulping and croaking?

They gulp as they breathe, because – unlike us – they have to force air into their lungs by swallowing it. The croaking is actually frog song. They use it to attract mates, mark their territory or just chat about the weather!

Frogs swallow air to breathe?
Wait a minute – do frogs have lungs,
or gills, or what?

Both. And most of them can breathe through their skin too.

What?

It's true. Frogs, newts and salamanders make up the larger part of the class **Amphibia** – the first group of vertebrates that evolved to live both in and out of the water. Within this class, newts and salamanders form the order **Caudata** (meaning 'tailed ones'), while frogs and toads are of the order **Anura** (or 'tail-less ones'). You can probably guess why.

Amphibia actually means 'both lives' in Greek, which nicely describes their habitat-hopping habits.

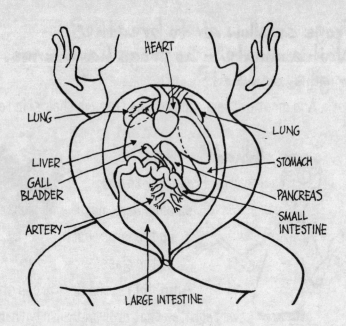

Frogs and toads breathe through their skin and gills as young tadpoles, living solely in the water. But as they develop legs they also develop air sacs, or lungs. In adult frogs and toads, these take over most of the breathing duties — although they also continue to breathe through their skin. This is part of the reason why frogs and toads tend to live in wet or watery places, like ponds, rivers and rainforests —

The female Argentinian Darwin's frog (Rhinoderma darwinii) actually lays its eggs in the forest, and the male picks them up and carries them around in his chin (or vocal) pouch! The eggs hatch into tadpoles inside, and the father spits them out into the water when they're half grown.

they have to keep their skin moist so that oxygen can dissolve into it from the air. The other reason, of course, is that most frogs and toads lay their eggs in the water.

What about newts – can they breathe through their skin too?

With newts and salamanders, it's a bit more complicated. While pretty much all of them can breathe through their skin, some have lungs, while others do not.

Most newts and salamanders have feathery external gills as young. These later turn into internal gills, which the adult animals continue to use in the water throughout life.

Get It Sorted – Strange Salamanders

The ghostly Mexican axolotl keeps its feathery external gills even as an adult, so it spends its whole life looking like an adult-sized baby.

To get some idea of how unusual this is — imagine if you were a six-foot adult human with the same long body, short limbs and huge, bald, outsized head you had as a baby. That's how weird the axolotl probably looks to other salamanders!

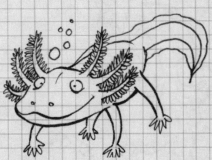

Some salamanders develop lungs, lose their gills and yet remain living in the water. To breathe, they have to surface for air like coastal dolphins. Others, meanwhile, lack both lungs and gills, and spend their whole lives on land, breathing only through their slimy skin. In a dry spell, these guys are really in trouble – because if their skin dries out they can't breathe, and quickly suffocate.

All of these strange and wonderful habits, of course, offer clues as to how these animals evolved. Amphibians have the longest history of all vertebrate animals. Modern frogs, toads, newts and salamanders all evolved from fleshy, lobe-finned fish over 200 million years ago, just as the dinosaurs were taking over the land. Reptiles and mammals evolved from a group of land-based, newt-like animals with lungs, that started spending more and more of their life cycles on land.

HOP!

At least one biologist has suggested that frogs evolved their high-speed hopping in order to escape hungry dinosaurs!

Good job too.

What do you mean?

Well, if it had been from one of the other groups, we'd have to breathe through our skin instead!

Actually, animals as large as us could never breathe through our skins alone. Our larger bodies need more oxygen than smaller animals, so we need a larger surface area to exchange oxygen and waste gases. Our lungs, thankfully, provide that extra area for us. If you unfolded all the tiny branching tubes and sacs inside our lungs, it would have roughly the same surface area as a tennis court.

Yeah – and if we did have to breathe through our skins, we wouldn't be able to wear clothes, or we'd suffocate. So everyone would be in the nude all the time. Even your parents!

Urrghhh!

Er . . . right.

So are frog lungs the same as ours, then?

Not quite. Ours differ from those of frogs and other air-breathing amphibians in that we have **lung muscles** – the most important being the large, flat diaphragm muscle that sits beneath them. With this, we can expand the twin air sacs in our chests to draw in air.

A frog, however, lacks these lung muscles. So it uses its mouth and throat muscles instead. To take a breath, the frog sucks air into its closed mouth through its nostrils, and then swallows the air to force it into the lungs. It does this by lowering and raising the floor of its mouth, which also makes the frog look like it's 'gulping' or swallowing something every few seconds.

Well, that explains all the gulping. But what about the croaking?

In a way, that's tied to the breathing. Many frog species have a large, stretchy vocal sac below their mouths. This sac can expand like a balloon and draw in extra air when the frog takes a deep breath in. By contracting muscles in the sac, the frog can shift the air to and from the lungs via the throat, vibrating its vocal cords on the way past. This is what makes the croak or 'ribbit' sound frogs are so famous for.

Very few species of frog actually go 'ribbit'. The reason why we link this sound to frogs is because one common frog species in the USA, in California, makes it. Sound engineers working on early Hollywood movies began recording sound clips of local frogs, for movie 'background' noises in films featuring swamps or jungles. And the same clips have been reused for years. So most of us think frogs go 'ribbit' because that's what movie frogs sound like!

But by contracting and vibrating their vocal sacs and vocal cords in different ways, different species of frog can produce hugely different sounds instead. Some sound like bells, gongs or whistles — others sound like dripping taps, burps, car horns or clarinets! In the rainforests of Brazil or Borneo, there are so many frog sounds at night that it sounds like a full froggy orchestra is playing, all night long.

Except you don't get many orchestras with whistlers and burpers sitting next to the violins and clarinets.

True. But if you did they could play a little Toad-zart, perhaps.

Groan.

Or perhaps some Newt-hoven.

Animal Categories

Test your vertebrate knowledge
by naming a species
for each starting letter.

The first line (all vertebrates starting with the
letter 'F') has been done for you. Now fill in the
blank lines by naming an animal starting with
the letter indicated for each of the five major
categories of backboned animals.

Letter	Fish	Amphibian
F	Flounder	Frog
S		
T	Tuna	
C		Cane toad
R	Ray	
G		
A		Axolotl

Good grief.

Dun-dun-dun-DUNNNN (ribbit).

Now play against your friends by naming a letter each round, and seeing who can think of the most animals (of any category) beginning with that letter in thirty seconds. You can either jot them down on paper, or – if you're in a car, on a journey – just shout them out and keep score that way. But don't shout too loud – you'll annoy your parents. Unless of course you get them to join in too . . .

Reptile	Bird	Mammal
Frilled lizard	Fulmar	Fox
		Skunk
	Thrush	
		Raccoon
	Gannet	
Alligator		

Dino-stories!

Could the dinosaurs ever come back?

Some of them never left! Many small dinosaurs didn't actually go extinct. They evolved into the birds you see around you every day. As for the others, it seems unlikely. It is currently impossible to clone them, *Jurassic Park*-style, from ancient DNA. And, even if we could, the modern world would be a tough place for a dinosaur to live.

Most books usually translate dinosaur as 'terrible lizard', but it's actually closer to 'awesome lizard'.

They never left? You mean they're still here?

In a way, yes. You see, not all of the dinosaurs died. And many of the large reptiles that did die were not actually dinosaurs, anyway.

Eh?

Let me explain.

The word 'dinosaur' comes from two Greek words meaning 'fearfully great lizard'. It describes two major groups of reptile that lived between 205 million and 65 million years ago. These two groups are the *ornithischian* (or 'bird-hipped') dinosaurs and the *saurischian* (or 'lizard-hipped') dinosaurs. As you may have gathered, these groups are named after the shapes of their hip bones, and whether they're shaped more like a bird's (tilted backwards) or like a lizard's (tilted forward). Got it?

Got it.

Good.

Get It Sorted – Bird-hipped v Lizard-hipped Dinosaurs

ornithischian dinos (plant eaters)	saurischian dinos	
	sauropods (four-legged plant eaters)	**therapods** (two-legged meat eaters)
Stegosaurus		
	Diplodocus	Velociraptor
Ankylosaurus		
	Apatosaurus	Tyrannosaurus rex
Triceratops		
	Brachiosaurus	Gigantosaurus
Iguanodon		

But the dinosaurs weren't the only large reptiles around. In the air, there were the flying **pterosaurs** (including the famous Pterodactyl).

In the oceans, the Nessie-like **plesiosaurs** and dolphin-like **ichthyosaurs**. And on land, the sail-backed Dimetrodon and others.

So they're not dinosaurs, then?

Nope. Most people mistake them for dinosaurs, but technically they're not. They're just large prehistoric reptiles. In any case, together, these all-powerful reptiles ruled the Earth for over 150 million years. But sadly most of them went the same way at the end of the Cretaceous period, around 65 million years ago.

So what happened?
How did they die?

As far as we can tell, most of the
dinosaurs were offed by a whole
series of events that happened
during the late Cretaceous
period. This included
massive volcanic
eruptions, a number
of impacts from
enormous
asteroids
(one of which
smashed into the ocean close to the coast of Mexico),
and a period of rapid, catastrophic climate change.

Whatever the case, by the end of the Cretaceous period, most
of the dinosaurs — along with four-fifths of the world's plants,
a third of its mammals and up to 65% of all animal species
worldwide — were gone. However, they didn't disappear at
once. Some struggled on for thousands of years, and while
pretty much all of the **ornithischians** went extinct,
a good number of the **saurischian** therapod dinosaurs
survived and evolved.

Wait a minute – that's the group that includes Velociraptors and Tyrannosaurus rex, right?

Right.

Wicked! So where are they?

Sadly, the largest therapods all died. But some of the smaller ones evolved feathers and, eventually, wings. So while most of the prehistoric world's large reptiles died, a good number of the **saurischians** live on through their modern descendants – birds.

Really? Like chickens, and sparrows, and ostriches?

Really. If you think about it, it isn't such a stretch. Just watch a chicken or ostrich walk some time. Look at its scaly legs and clawed feet, imagine it without feathers, and bang – there it is . . . a mini *Velociraptor*.

Get It Sorted – How Did Birds Learn to Fly?

The development of flight has been a mystery since before the time of Darwin, and scientists can't say for sure exactly which route early birds took to the air, but they think those early fliers formed two camps: the **daredevil drop-gliders** and the **ground-running jump-flappers.**

Jump-flappers

Birds evolved from small therapod dinosaurs. These reptiles were featherless, wingless and ran along the ground on two legs (like an ostrich or roadrunner) to catch prey and escape predators. Then some of these dinosaurs mutated and grew feathers on their bodies and forelimbs. At first these probably just helped to keep them warm. But later they took on a different purpose . . .

Sometimes, when being chased by a predator, these early dino-birds would have to run and jump over obstacles, climb slopes or claw their way up vertical tree trunks to escape. If the mutant, feathered ground-runners flapped their stubby arms as they did this, perhaps they could gain a bit more height, and survive better than animals without these feathered 'winglets', so natural selection would favour them over no winglets at all. Over time, dinosaurs with bigger, stronger winglets would evolve. Then, eventually, they would develop full-size working wings and learn to leave the ground altogether – as flapping, flying birds.

Drop-gliders

Some of those early feathered dino-birds may have started climbing tall trees, launching themselves off and then parachuting or gliding down to the ground (to find new food sources, or to escape from predators). It might sound like a lot of effort, but other animals – like sugar-gliders and flying squirrels – are already known to do just that. Both these mammals have flaps of skin that stretch from their hands to their feet, forming a thin, fleshy, hang-glider or parachute that can carry them for long distances in the air.

The giant Asian flying squirrel and marsupial greater glider can glide over 100 m (300 feet) or more!

Whether they evolved as jump-flappers or drop-gliders, birds have come a long way since then. While many other animals have evolved many types of flight, birds are definitely the most accomplished aeronauts.

Yeah, yeah. But a chicken-sized dinosaur is hardly very scary, is it?

Up until the seventeenth century, you could have seen a much larger, scarier dino-descendant on the island of Madagascar. The 3m (10-foot) tall, flightless elephant bird was about half the size of a Stegosaurus, but still big enough to maim or kill you with a well-aimed kick. Sadly, this wasn't enough to protect it from human hunters, who chased it to extinction around 400 years ago.

Seeing one of those would be pretty smart, I s'pose. But why did all the big ones have to die? I mean, they were so cool. And if other big lizards like crocodiles are as old as the dinosaurs, how come the dinosaurs died but they didn't?

We don't know for certain, but it's fairly safe to say that crocs were somehow better adapted to survive the changes that happened around 65 million years ago, when most of the dinosaurs disappeared. It may have been to do with size and competition. Larger animals need larger food supplies, so perhaps reptiles larger than crocodiles had a harder time finding enough food.

Large reptiles also find it more difficult to regulate their body temperatures (which is why crocodiles and alligators only live in tropical or sub-tropical areas). Without fur or feathers, the larger dinosaurs may have had more trouble – compared to crocs and smaller reptiles – in keeping warm during the colder winters that followed the asteroid strike, volcanic eruptions and climate change. This, then, might also explain why some of the smaller ones evolved feathers and became birds — not, in the beginning, for flight . . . but for warmth.

Whatever the reason, we do know this: if the dinosaurs were to come back today, they'd find a very different world to the one they evolved to live in — a world in which it would be very tough for them to survive and thrive.

Get It Sorted – Dino Facts

* The vast majority of dinosaurs were herbivores (plant-eaters), rather than carnivores.
* The famous Tyrannosarus rex was not, in fact, the largest carnivorous dinosaur. The largest known T. rex measured 13 m (42 feet) long, and weighed over 6 tonnes. But at 18 m (60 feet) long and weighing in at almost 10 tonnes, the terrifying sail-backed Spinosaurus would have towered over it. Luckily for T. rex, Spinosaurus lived thousands of years earlier, so they never met.
* Many dinosaurs were feathered, and some were probably quite brightly coloured, like modern-day peacocks and parrots.
* Male Velcociraptors had feathery 'top-knot' hairstyles, which they probably used to attract picky females.

RRRAAARR!

But dinosaurs are well tough! Nothing could beat a dinosaur. They're tougher than anything!

Maybe. But, then again, maybe not. For one thing, they evolved and conquered the Earth largely in the absence of mammals. But when the dinosaurs died off, the mammals filled all their niches and replaced them in the food chains. Left to compete with ruthless, egg-eating mammals today, they might not do so well.

Nor are dinosaurs tougher than the climate. During the late Cretaceous period when the dinosaurs last lived, the climate was much warmer. There were no ice caps at the poles, and dinosaurs migrated back and forth between warm, wet North America, Africa, Asia and Europe, and a pleasantly cool Russia, Canada and Greenland. Sixty-five million years later, the air is thinner, the plants are different and the world — despite steadily increasing temperatures thanks to global warming — is generally a lot cooler.

It was a rapidly changing climate and environment that spelled the end of the dinosaurs in the first place. Thrust them back into the world now and the chances are they wouldn't last too long.

All right – but what if we could clone them? And what if global warming heated up the world so much that it was better suited to dinosaurs than mammals? And what if they busted out of all the science labs and scoffed all the mammals, including us? Then would dinosaurs rule the world again?

That's a lot of what ifs . . . but it's possible, I suppose.

That's good enough for me!

Wait a minute – do you actually want to be eaten by a dinosaur?

Who cares? Dinosaurs RULE!

RRRRRAAAAAAAA!

(Sigh.)

WE MIGHTY MAMMALS

Let me tell you a story . . . the story of a great battle.

The time – the Cretaceous period, over 65 million years ago.

The place – planet Earth, but not as we know it.

For over 150 million years, ravenous reptiles – large and small – had ruled the Earth. At their feet scampered the tiny, insignificant mammals. But soon this was all to change . . .

Great volcanoes erupted, spewing fire
and sulphur into the atmosphere. Huge
boulders rained down from the skies,
smashing into the Earth and throwing
up vast dust clouds that blotted out

the sun for months at a time. The climate shifted, bringing
colder, drier winters that killed off all but the hardiest
animals.

The Great Lizards
were tested, and most
struggled to survive.
But at their feet the
mammals found ways
to survive and thrive.

The remaining reptiles and the rising ranks of mammals fought
a final battle for dominion over the land.

In the end, the mammals emerged victorious and spread
throughout the world, ever to rule the reptiles as kings among
the vertebrates. The mammals had inherited the Earth, and
the Age of Reptiles was no more.

THE END

Or, rather . . .

THE BEGINNING

Because THAT, my friends, is how we mighty mammals came to be the great, world-altering class of animals we are today — from the tiniest shrew to the tallest giraffe, the strongest elephant, the most enormous whale and the cleverest human.*

Now, together, let's take our final trip, to meet the rulers of the vertebrate world.

If all mammals make milk, do kangaroos make milkshakes?

Kangaroo mothers do make milk, but sadly no amount of hopping and bouncing will turn it into a milkshake for their young joeys. That said, plain old mammalian milk is pretty amazing stuff all by itself.

Glenn Murphy

* *Me.* Obviously.

No milkshakes, then? Pity. I thought maybe it could lob a couple of strawberries or bananas into the pouch, and . . .

Sadly, no. Aside from the fact that strawberries and bananas don't grow in the hot, dry Australian Outback, kangaroo milk isn't made in the pouch, anyway. (That's just where the joeys receive it). Nice idea, though.

Sigh. All right, then – what's so great about plain old mammal's milk?

Being mammals ourselves, we tend to take milk for granted. But, if you think about it, it's truly amazing stuff. It's a delicious, nutritious, mobile food — one that baby mammals can survive on for months or even years, in the absence of anything else. Along with a few other special features, the ability to produce milk is part of what defines mammals.

It's also one of three secret weapons that gave mammals the edge in that age-old battle with their prehistoric rivals – the reptiles – that we just heard about in the intro to this chapter.

Yeah, that was very exciting and all, but I didn't quite get one thing.

What was that?

How did the mammals manage to survive and beat the reptiles, when they started out so small and puny?

Ahh – good question. With new tactics for survival. Which is where kangaroo pouches and mammalian milk come in . . .

SECRET WEAPON #1

Mammals, you see, were the first animals to give birth to live young. Reptiles, by contrast, lay eggs. In general, laying eggs means staying put, or nesting, and reptile parents have to protect their defenceless, immobile young while they slowly develop inside the eggs, or risk losing them to egg-eating animals. Even the dinosaurs had to do this.

But mammals found a way around this weakness. Giving birth to live young allowed mammals to stay on the move, taking their weak, toddling (but mobile) babies with them as they looked for food or hid from predators. Some mammals, like kangaroos, wallabies and possums (the marsupials) went one better by evolving pouches in which to keep their babies. This allowed them to reproduce faster, by giving birth to babies that were little more than embryos, then safely transporting and nursing them in the pouch until they were big enough to walk and follow their mother.

Some possums even have waterproof pouches, which they can snap shut while swimming to keep their young safe and dry inside.

Okay, so pouches were a plus for some mammals. But how did milk help?

SECRET WEAPON #2

Milk enabled mammals to feed their weak, undeveloped, vulnerable young while living life on the move. As embryos, egg-laying animals feed off the nutrients in the egg's yolk. If they're lucky — and the egg isn't scoffed first — they hatch as weak, puny babies. They then mature slowly into adults, largely unguarded by their parents, who have to spend most of their time away, looking for food. (Just think of a bird leaving its nest to fetch worms. Not all reptiles look after their young that well — many abandon their young soon after hatching — but you get the idea.) This leaves the babies at risk of attack, even after they're born.

Mammals, on the other hand, have milk-producing mammary glands (or at least the females do). This turns them into mobile food dispensers, churning out litres and litres of high-protein, high-vitamin, 'super-gro' baby food on the move. This constant supply of liquid wonder-grub allows the babies to grow and mature very quickly, making them more likely to survive to adulthood.

Kangaroo mothers, amazingly, can produce three different types of milk – with different amounts of fat and nutrients – to feed joeys of different ages at the same time. One tiny, day-old joey may be suckling one type of milk deep inside the pouch, while another three-month-old joey hops beneath the mother to receive a different milk formula from another teat. So kangaroo mums have milk-making down to a fine art.

So that's what allowed the mammals to win out over the reptiles? Milk power?

Mostly, yes. But mammals also had one more trick up their sleeves. Or, rather, on their bodies.

Hair.

SECRET WEAPON #3

Hair?

Yep — **hair**. With very few
exceptions, all mammals are
hairy or furry. But there's not
an amphibian or reptile in the
world with a patch of the stuff.
They have scales instead, and
lack the special cells from

which hair follicles grow. Hair not only makes mammals look
nice and cuddly, it also keeps them warm and cosy. Hair — and
the thick mats of it we call *fur* — traps a layer of warm air next
to an animal's body, helping to insulate it and retain body heat
in cold environments.

Reptiles lack this insulation,
and have to bask in sunlight
during the day (and roost
at night) to maintain their
body temperature. We say
that they're cold-blooded, or
ectothermic ('outside-heated').

Wish you were here!

Mammals, on the other hand, are warm-blooded, or *endothermic* ('inside-heated'). They produce more body heat at rest, and maintain their body temperature at roughly the same level all day (and night) long. Having a hairy or furry coat (along with more layers of body fat) helps mammals to do this by insulating them.

So their warm blood, extra fat and insulating coats allowed mammals to do lots of things reptiles couldn't. Like hunt at night while most reptiles were curled up, motionless, to conserve energy. Or spread into colder, cloudier regions of the world – like the Arctic, Antarctica and high mountain tops – where cold-blooded reptiles simply could not survive.

Brrrrr!

And that's why there are polar bears and Arctic foxes, but no snow snakes or ice lizards?

Exactly. We warm, hairy, milky mammals can chill out in places where reptiles would only chill to death.

Yeah, but if we could make our own milkshakes, then we'd really be chillin'.

Well, we can. We just have to use electric blenders to do it. Sadly, we're unlikely to evolve the ability to produce milkshakes, since we can happily survive without them.

I can't!

Fine. Go make one with a blender, then. See? Mammals can make milkshakes!

GLUG! GLUG!

Marsupial Crossword

Across

1   Looks like a cross between a beaver and a mallard (4, 6, 8)

Down

2   The world's largest marsupial (3, 8)

3   Like a wee kangaroo (7)

4   Toothy, long-extinct beast whose Latin name was *Thylacoleo carnifex* (13)

5   Eucalyptus-loving tree-climber, often mistaken for a bear (5)

6   The only marsupial native to North America (7)

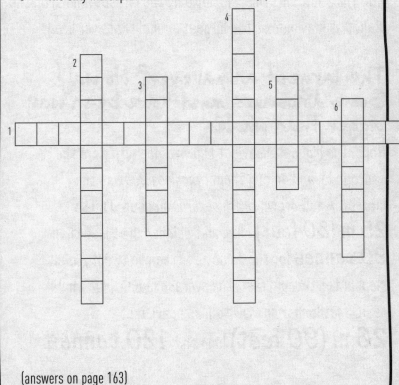

(answers on page 163)

How BIG does a whale baby get?

The largest, a blue whale calf, can be **8 m (24 feet)** in length at birth, and weigh over **three tonnes** – or roughly the same size and weight as a large transit

CREAK!

van. The adult blue whale is not only the largest animal on the planet, it may also be the largest animal that ever lived.

The largest animal ever? No way! Some dinosaurs must have been way bigger than whales.

Nope. The biggest, heaviest known dinosaurs were the sauropods, and among them *Brachiosaurus* was the largest. A full-grown *Brachiosaurus* measured up to **25 m (80 feet)** long, and weighed in at less than **90 tonnes** (or the same as fifteen to twenty adult elephants). By contrast, the average female blue whale is 10 feet longer and 30 tonnes heavier, at **26 m (90 feet)** long and **120 tonnes**.

Whoa. That is pretty heavy.

That's nothing. The *largest* blue whale on record was **30 m (100 feet)** long, and weighed almost **200 tonnes**. That's almost twice as much as a Brachiosaurus.

So how did they get so big? Whales, I mean, not dinosaurs. Although those too, I suppose . . .

Both probably evolved their enormous bulk as a defence against predators. Basically, the larger you are, the fewer predators you're likely to have. There weren't too many things that could take on a *Brachiosaurus* in the prehistoric world. Nor are there many things around today (besides humans) that can kill a large whale. But while most land animals are limited in size by the amount of body weight they can support and shift with their legs, whales take advantage of their salt-water home to support their huge bodies.

How do they do that?

By floating. Although incredibly heavy, a whale's body is still buoyant, meaning it can displace enough water to float.

So using the water to support their weight has allowed whales to grow larger than they could have on land. And while the largest land animals, African bush elephants, stand up to **4 m (12 feet)** tall and weigh **4–7 tonnes**, many whales reach *considerably* larger sizes. Check out the list below.

Weight There, Animal!

Animal	Length (in metres)	Weight (in tonnes)	Weight (in elephants)
African elephant	4	5	1
Killer whale	10	10	2
Humpback whale	14	40	8
Sperm whale	18	45	9
Blue whale	26	120	24

So, many whales are *many times* larger than even the largest of land animals. But they weren't always that big. In fact, they *couldn't* get that big until after they'd made their way back to the sea.

'Back' to the sea?

Right. Back. Because whales — as you know — are mammals. And, like all other mammals, they descended from fish and amphibians that left the water to make their lives on land. There, their ancestors evolved legs, lungs, warm blood, fur and mammary glands. Only later did they walk back into swamps and shallow seas, lose their legs and evolve back into aquatic animals. The whole journey from sea to land and back again took over 300 million years. But by the Tertiary era, around 15 million years after the extinction of most dinosaurs, early whales were happily swimming the prehistoric oceans.

Whales had legs once? Weird. What did they look like?

Whales, dolphins and porpoises form the family of animals known as cetaceans, whose closest living relatives on land are probably hippos. But their earliest known ancestors are from the group **archaeoceti** (or 'the ancient whales'), which lived in freshwater rivers and swamps over 50 million years ago. They had four stubby (but working) legs, and probably trotted between the land and water while hunting, breeding and avoiding large predators. But in their hind legs, the thigh (or femur) bone grew smaller, and they were already starting to look more streamlined and whale-like.

Ambulocetus ('walking whale'), another ancient whale ancestor, was about the size of a modern sea lion, and probably moved in much the same way. In the water, it would ripple its spine to swim, with its webbed feet trailing behind it, while on land it would walk with its front limbs, dragging its weaker hind limbs behind it.

Of these two, modern-day whales and dolphins probably evolved from **archaeoceti**, eventually losing their hind limbs altogether and evolving flukes (or fins) on the ends of their tails that would propel them through the water. Their nostrils also moved to the tops of their heads, forming a blow-hole through which the whale could breathe without lifting its whole head out of the water.

Perhaps the most impressive thing about cetaceans is their intelligence. **Humpback whales** migrate tens of thousands of miles across the world's oceans, using rumbling, infrasonic whalesong to talk to each other over distances of 2,000 miles (3,000 km) or more.

Dolphins, meanwhile, hunt fish in packs — communicating with each other using rapid ultrasonic clicks. In tests, dolphins have shown true problem-solving intelligence, and can recognize their own images in mirrors or video displays. And they're well known for their playful, curious natures — often playing with swimmers or divers for hours on end.

Really? I wanna play! Where can I swim with a dolphin, or spot a whale out at sea?

For now, lots of places. But unless we protect them from being struck by ships, caught in fishing nets or harpooned by whaling fleets, they won't be around forever. Many species of whale and dolphin are already endangered, and one — the Chinese river dolphin — went extinct just a few years ago.

Wow. They spend 300 million years surviving the land and sea, and then we come along with a big fishing boat. Doesn't seem fair.

It's not. And that's exactly why we need to look after them. After all – they're graceful, they're playful, they're intelligent and – above all else – they're family.

Aqua-mammal Anagrams

Unravel these anagrams, and reveal eight different species of cetacean mammal.

Rise poop   _ _ _ _ _ _ _ _

Garth while   _ _ _ _ _ _ _ _ _ _

Law hub eel   _ _ _ _ _ _ _ _ _

Maple shrew   _ _ _ _ _ _ _ _ _ _

Warlike hell   _ _ _ _ _ _ _ _ _ _ _

Bootes lent hold pin   _ _ _ _ _ _ _ _ _ _ _ _ _ _ _ _ _

Lawn rah   _ _ _ _ _ _ _

Pinch mold moon   _ _ _ _ _ _ _ _ _ _ _ _

(answers on page 163)

Do tigers purr?

No. At least not like your pet cat does. Tigers and other big cats have different bone structures in their throats to smaller cats. So while tigers, lions and leopards can make rumbling noises in their throats, they can only do it while breathing out — not continuously like your house-kitty can. On the other hand, almost all big cats can roar, which is a far more useful noise for life in the wild.

ROAR!

So big cats don't really purr? Why not?

Because although they're all in the same family of mammals, the *Felidae*, and they all share common ancestors, big cats and domestic cats have evolved different 'voices' — each suited to their lifestyles. And big cats, it seems, may have traded in their ability to make a constant *prrrr, prrr* in favour of a much louder (and scarier)

RRRAAWWWWWWRRRR!

PURRRRRRRRRR! **I'M IN PAIN**

GRRPURRRRRRRR! **I'M ANGRY**

PURRRRRRR !!! **I'M NERVOUS**

PURRRRRRR :) **I'M HAPPY!**

How did that happen?

Well, domestic cats and other small cats (of the genus *Felis*) have a solid hyoid bone in their throats, which supports their tongue and vocal muscles. As air flows back and forth across this bone with each inhale and exhale, the hyoid (along with the vocal muscles) vibrate, creating a continuous prrrrrrrrrrrr sound. Cats, as you may have gathered, use purring for communication.

Like, to tell you they're happy?

Amongst other things, yes. But different pitches of purr — from a deep rumble to a high trill — can also mean different things, such as 'I'm nervous', 'I'm angry' or even 'I'm in pain'.

Oh. I didn't know that. So if tigers can't purr, how are you supposed to know if they're happy, nervous, angry or what?

Well, frankly, even if they could purr, would you want to risk getting close enough to listen?

Er . . . no. Good point.

Right. And nor would most animals. Including other tigers. Which may be one reason why big cats have evolved a more long-distance alternative. In most big cats (of the genus *Panthera*), the hyoid bone has elastic sections that can slide and stretch like a trombone as exhaled air blasts its way past. On the downside, this doesn't provide enough solid support for a continuous purr. On the upside, it does (along with the vocal muscles) allow them to create a faster, harder, louder vibration, otherwise known as a **ROAR!**

And they use that to scare off other cats, right?

Right. Big cats can roar out warnings at a distance of
5 miles (8 km) or more. But, as
smaller cats do with purrs,
they also use roars closer
up to attract mates,
or express anger,
nervousness or pain.

So while small cats
can purr but not roar, most big cats can roar but not purr.
Similarly, while dogs (*Canidae*) and bears (*Ursidae*) are quite
closely related, dogs can bark but not roar while bears can
roar but not bark.

Dogs and bears are related?

Yep. In fact, dogs, bears and cats are all part of a larger order of mammals called **Carnivora**.

Which means 'meat-eaters', right?

Right. But while the word 'carnivor'e means 'anything that eats meat' (and so includes many reptiles, birds, and even one or two plants!), Carnivora refers only to eleven or so families of mostly meat-eating mammals. (Triple 'M's, if you like!) Many biologists, though, use these two words interchangeably. So we will too.

Not all carnivores always hunt and eat meat. Some, like hyenas and raccoons, are mostly scavengers, rather than hunters. And others – like pandas and aardwolves – feed on plants, fish, insects or a mixture of these.

How many kinds of carnivore are there?

If we're talking Carnivora, there are about 270 species, arranged into 11 families. These include:

- **Felidae** (domestic cats, wild cats, jungle cats, lions, tigers, leopards, jaguars, panthers, pumas)

- **Canidae** (dogs, wolves, dingoes)

- **Hyaenadae** (hyenas, aardwolves)

- **Ursidae** (bears)

- **Procyonidae** (raccoons, kinkajous)

- **Mustelidae** (weasels, minks, skunks, otters)

- **Herpestidae** (mongooses, meerkats)

- **Viverridae** (civets, genets, binturongs)

Many of these you may never have heard of. Civets and genets, for example, look like large, dog-sized weasels or meerkats, and live throughout Africa and South-east Asia. Binturongs (otherwise known as bear-cats) look like massive all-black racoons with long, muscular tails. They, too, live in the forests of South-east Asia. Though you don't hear

Binturongs use their tail to grip trees and hang upside down from tree branches. They also, strangely, smell like popcorn.

about (or see) them much, civets, genets and binturongs may well be closest in appearance to miacids, the first mammalian carnivores, which evolved a few million years after most of the dinosaurs copped it at the end of the Cretaceous period. From these strange animals, all modern cats, dogs, bears and other Carnivora have since evolved and spread around the world.

The Human Animal

Are human beings animals, apes or just people?

We're all three! Like all other mammal species, we humans are hairy, warm-blooded, give birth to live young and nurse them with self-made milk. Like all other primates (which includes both apes and monkeys), humans have keen vision, forward-facing eyes and thumb joints that let us grip things. And although we've lost much of our hair and fur, and our brains have some extra bits, we're more similar to our distant mammal cousins than we sometimes like to think.

Oh, come on. There are loads of things that make us different from apes and monkeys. We're *nothing* like them.

Okay . . . like what kinds of things?

Well, their bodies are all hairy. All over.

True, but up until quite recently, so were we. Some of our hominid (or human-like) ancestors, like *Australopithecus*, were every bit as hairy as any ape or monkey. It's only been 5 million years since they walked the plains of Africa. And even now we are

152

still hairy animals. Especially as adult males. It's just that the hair has become thinner and lighter — only remaining thick and heavy in certain places on the body, like the head, face, armpits and groin.

All right, then – what about walking? And talking? And using tools? And we're much cleverer.

That's true, we are cleverer. And no other primate can talk, either. But we're actually not the only ones that can walk on two legs. Nor are we the only primates that use tools. It's just that we do these things a lot better than the others.

Really? There are walking and tool-using apes out there somewhere? Other than us, I mean.

Yes — there really are. And, if you think about it, it makes perfect sense. After all, we already know that at the end of the Cretaceous period, the only mammals on the planet were little shrew-like animals scampering at the feet of the ailing dinosaurs. Yet here we are today, 65 million years later, as walking, talking, tool-using, super-smart mammals. Therefore, we had to have evolved these features and abilities at some point in between. And if you follow the history of the primates, by looking at the families still with us today, you can see how it all happened.

So how did it happen?

Thought you'd never ask . . .

It all began about 65 million years ago...

with those little four-legged scampering, shrew-mammals. Some of them evolved into the weasel-like miacids, which eventually led to the carnivores. Others evolved into the hoofed ungulates (hoofed mammals like horses), toothy rodents and rabbits, flippered dolphins and whales and flapping bats.

But one group took to the trees, evolving longer limbs and grasping hands to help them leap and climb between lofty branches. These animals would have looked a lot like today's **prosimians** (meaning 'before-monkeys'), which include lemurs, lorises and bushbabies.

Animals like this were the very first primates. Like us, they have opposable (or backward-facing) thumbs, which means they can grip tree branches and hold pieces of fruit while they eat them.

Big deal. So can squirrels.

Squirrels don't eat fruit.

You know what I mean.

Okay, fine. If you're not impressed by that, then get this. Lemurs and 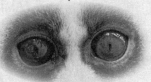 lorises also have two large, forward-facing eyes, which gives them overlapping, stereoscopic vision. With these, they can accurately judge distances between branches — which obviously comes in handy if you need to jump to survive. Lemurs also, occasionally, stand upright on two legs and skip.

Not bad. But that's still not walking or using tools. Nothing like it.

Right, for that we have to wait another 30 million years, for the evolution of monkeys and apes. By 35 million years ago, the ancestors of monkeys, gorillas, chimps and humans were swinging and knuckle-walking their way through the ancient forests of Africa, Asia and South America.

With better-developed brains, eyes and limbs, these animals learned to use their hands in more complex ways, developing hand dexterity. One group of these animals eventually led to the monkeys, marmosets and gibbons — who stayed high in the trees to feed on fruits and avoid predators on the ground. But another evolved into the **hominoids** (or 'human-likes'). This family includes gorillas, chimps, orang-utans and humans.

Hominoids all have enlarged brains, dexterous hands and — apparently — the ability to make and use tools.

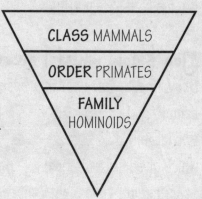

CLASS MAMMALS

ORDER PRIMATES

FAMILY
HOMINOIDS

No way! What kind of tool does a chimp use?

Actually, chimps make and use lots of them, including rocks (hammers for cracking nuts), sticks and stones (weapons to ward off leopards and rivals), and thin twigs (to fish insects and grubs out of hollow trees and termite mounds).

And while gorillas and orang-utans aren't often seen using tools in the wild, they will use many of the same tools as chimps if given a food-related problem to solve in captivity. Gorillas, chimps and orang-utans can also easily learn to walk upright if trained. In the wild, they have mainly stuck to knuckle-walking, since the thick underbrush of the forest prevents them from standing up.

That is pretty impressive, I suppose. But they still can't walk or talk like us.

True, they can't. There are limits to what gorillas and chimps can do. And that's because of one major thing we have that they don't — an expanded region of outer brain called the **cerebral cortex**. It's this that makes our species truly different from all the other primates — and unique among all the other mammals.

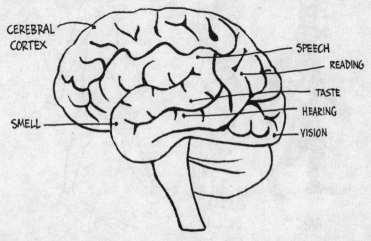

At some point, around 5 million years ago, our ancestors split off from those of chimpanzees and bonobos (pygmy chimpanzees). And when they did their brains went through a biological **Big Bang**.

From early hominids like *Australopithecus* to *Homo habilis* ('handy man'), *Homo erectus* ('upright man'), and finally to our own species, *Homo sapiens* ('clever man'), our brains became more and more complex. With newly developed areas of the outer brain, and some extra rewiring throughout bits of the rest, we began to develop more and more sophisticated forms of body control – including the control of highly developed vocal muscles, that would later allow us to speak and communicate.

HABILIS   ERECTUS   SAPIENS

Get It Sorted – Big Brainy Bang

We don't know for sure what
caused the Big Brainy Bang.
Something drove the brain to
expand and develop in new ways, *which
gave our ancestors an advantage* in
survival. It may have been a demand
for more complex movements (or
motor skills) that came with balancing,
walking, running and jumping on two
legs. It may have been the need to
develop more hand dexterity, for crafting
tools like axes

and spear heads. It may have been the need to
communicate with each other in hunting, or in
teaching others how to craft weapons and tools.
Later, when our brains were
developed enough, we began to dance, sing and
produce simple artworks – like cave paintings
or carved wooden figures. At this point, perhaps
females started to prefer the better dancers,
singers and artists, and helped to select for
bigger, more creative brains . . .

Our brains and our intelligence is what makes our species, *Homo sapiens*, truly unique. But at the same time, recognizing our similarities to the other apes helps to remind us of what we have in common.

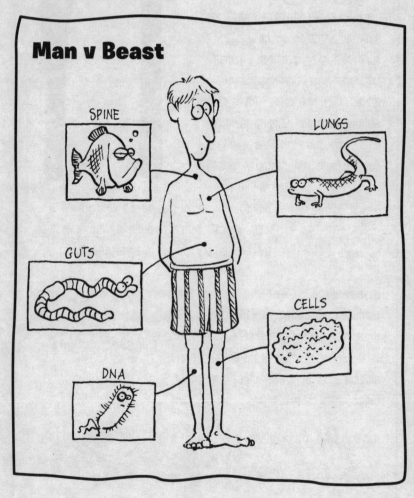

But I hope now that you see, also, that our links with the animal kingdom go much deeper — all the way to the air sacs we share with amphibians, the backbones we share with fish, the guts we share with worms, the cells we share with sponges, and the DNA we share with the many billions of bacteria that live in and around our bodies.

All forms of life are one — one wonderful union of living things, linked to each other through our shared evolutionary past.

Now, in the present, it's up to us to study, respect and protect all forms of life, so we can continue to enjoy each other's company well into the future.

So don't stop here — there's so much more to learn! Search your local and school library for books on zoology (preferably fun ones with lots of cool pictures). Visit websites and join conservation groups like the **World Wildlife Fund** (wwf.org.uk) to help protect rare and endangered animals.

Remember — humans are not just a part of the living world. We are also its caretakers. So listen, learn and look after your wondrous animal planet. Trust me — you'll be very glad you did.

ANSWERS

(page 30) **Animal Anagrams**

Spotted skunk; killer whale; grizzly bear;
red kangaroo; duck-billed platypus; giant panda

(page 36) **DIY Zoology**

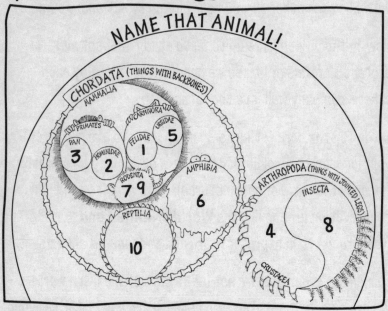

(page 38) **Spot the Hybrid**

Zeedonk, liger, jaglion, yakow and zorse are the real hybrids.

(page 56) Secret Weapon

Hyena/teeth, tiger/claws, warthog/tusks, ibex/antlers, bat/ultrasound, leaf mantis/camouflage, skunk/chemical spray, cobra/deadly venom, pangolin/body armour.

(page 84) Odd Bug Out

1. Millipede (the rest are insects)

2. Daddy long-legs (the rest are arachnids)

3. Cuttlefish (the rest are crustaceans)

4. Starfish (the rest are arthropods – yes, even the barnacle!)

(page 137) Marsupial Crossword

Across

1. Duck-billed platypus

Down

2. Red kangaroo; 3. Wallaby; 4. Marsupiallion; 5. Koala; 6. Opossum

(page 144) Aqua-mammal Anagrams

Porpoise; right whale; blue whale; sperm whale; killer whale; bottlenose dolphin; narwhal; common dolphin

Picture Credits

Websites

BBC Nature Page	www.bbc.co.uk/nature/animals/
Arkive	www.arkive.org
Zoological Society of London	www.zsl.org/kids/
Wildlife Trusts	www.wildlifetrusts.org/
National Geographic Animals	animals.nationalgeographic.com/animals/

Turn the page to read an exciting extract from

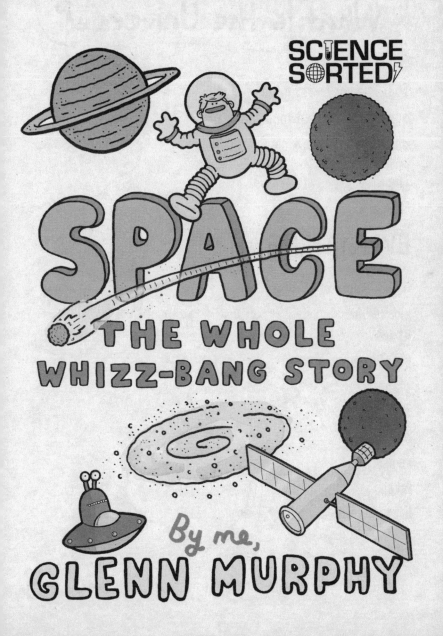

SCIENCE SORTED

SPACE

THE WHOLE WHIZZ-BANG STORY

By me,

GLENN MURPHY

Hang on a Minute – What Is the Universe?

That is a very, very good question. One that most people don't bother to ask.

The Universe is *all there is*. Literally.

EVERYTHING. All of it.

It contains everything from
vast galaxies,
stars,
black holes,
planets,
moons,
oceans,
rivers,
lakes,
land masses

. . . plus every single life-form that lives on (or in) them.

All there is? Like, EVERYTHING?

Yep. *Everything*. The word 'universe' comes from the Greek, meaning 'all together' or 'turned into one'. And as far as we know there's nothing beyond it. Cosmologists reckon it's billions of light years across and, since it's still expanding, it's getting bigger every day.

We also know that it's around 13.7 billion years old, and began life in a huge explosion of matter and energy known as the ...

Big Bang!

(They must have been up all night thinking up the name for that one.)

Before that there was nothing. No matter, no energy . . . no Space, even. The Bang created all these things as it went.

Get It Sorted – Light Year

A light year is the distance travelled by a particle of light, moving at the speed of light, in one Earth year. Since the speed of light is roughly 300 million metres per second (or 670 million miles per hour), that means a light year is roughly equal to about 9,500,000,000,000 (nine trillion, five hundred billion) kilometres, or 5,900,000,000,000 (five trillion, nine hundred million) miles. Or, put another way, 63,000 times the distance from the Earth to the Sun.

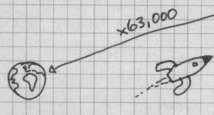

Now multiply that by 27,400,000,000, and that'll give you some idea of how big the Universe is (or at least the small part of it we can see – it's very probably much bigger!)

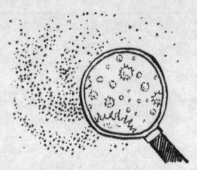

BIG NUMBERS ALERT!

We know that the Universe contains over 100 billion galaxies. Within each galaxy at least 70,000 million million million (or 70 sextillion) stars happily twinkle. Well, not so much twinkle as BURN.

Stars burn?

Yep. And, what's more, they burn brighter and hotter than anything on Earth. Stars, we've discovered, are not little twinkling dots in the dark curtain of the sky.

They are massive, ball-shaped nuclear reactors — giant spheres of hydrogen and helium gas burning and exploding with energy from nuclear reactions going on within them.

Yikes. That sounds a bit scary, actually. Massive nuclear reactors. Like . . . how massive?

Well, our own star — the Sun — is roughly 109 times wider than the Earth, and 330,000 times heavier. And that's not even one of the big ones. Some stars are 100 to 1,000 times wider *again*. They can get so massive, in fact, that they collapse in on themselves, then rebound with an explosion that burns a billion times brighter than the Sun — leaving behind an enormous, invisible hole in Space from which nothing can escape. What's more, a monstrous black hole like this could lie at the centre of our own galaxy, the Milky Way.

Get It Sorted – How Big Is the Universe?

Unlike galaxies and solar systems, the Universe has no single central point, and may have no edge. Physicists say it's quite possible that the Universe simply folds back on itself. So if you flew a spaceship in one direction for long enough, you would never actually reach the edge of the Universe. Just like flying an aeroplane around the world, you'd end up back where you started. Only billions of years older, and probably quite annoyed.

DISGUSTING SCIENCE

WHAT'S WORSE THAN FINDING A MAGGOT IN YOUR APPLE?
WHICH SMELLS WORSE: A ROTTEN EGG OR A ROTTEN LEG?
WHAT ARE SICK AND POO MADE OF?

GLENN MURPHY, AUTHOR OF *WHY IS SNOT GREEN?*,
ANSWERS THESE AND LOTS OF OTHER REVOLTING QUESTIONS
IN THIS HILARIOUS, FASCINATING AND INFORMATIVE BOOK.

PACKED WITH ILLUSTRATIONS, PHOTOGRAPHS AND FACTS
ABOUT ALL SORTS OF DISGUSTING THINGS, FROM BUGS,
BACTERIA AND SWEATY ARMPITS TO EXPLODING BODIES
AND CREEPY-CRAWLY CREATURES, THIS BOOK CONTAINS
ABSOLUTELY NO BORING BITS!

GLENN MURPHY